D0867016

DEBT AND DEVELOPMENT CRISES IN LATIN AMERICA:
THE END OF AN ILLUSION

DEBT AND DEVELOPMENT CRISES IN LATIN AMERICA THE END OF AN ILLUSION

STEPHANY GRIFFITH-JONES AND OSVALDO SUNKEL

CLARENDON PRESS · OXFORD

1986

Oxford University Press, Walton Street, Oxford OX2 6DP
Oxford New York Toronto
Delhi Bombay Calcutta Madras Karachi
Petaling Jaya Singapore Hong Kong Tokyo
Nairobi Dar es Salaam Cape Town
Melbourne Auckland
and associated companies in
Beirut Berlin Ibadan Nicosia

Oxford is a trade mark of Oxford University Press

Published in the United States
by Oxford University Press, New York

British Library Cataloguing in Publication Data
Griffith-Jones, Stephany
Debt and development crises in Latin
America: the end of an illusion.
1. Latin America—Economic conditions
I. Title II. Sunkel, Osvaldo
330.98 HC123
ISBN 0-19-828546-9

Library of Congress Cataloging-in-Publication Data
Griffith-Jones, Stephany.
Debt and development crisis in Latin America.
Bibliography: p.
1. Debts, External—Latin America. 2. Latin
America—Economic conditions—1945- . 3. Inter-
national finance. I. Sunkel, Osvaldo. II. Title.
HJ8514.5.G748 1986 336.3'435'098 86-16291
ISBN 0-19-828546-9

Set by Hope Services, Abingdon
Printed in Great Britain by
Billing & Sons Ltd
Worcester

To Raul Prebisch and Dudley Seers, who contributed so much to our understanding (and that of others) of the links between national development and the international economy

Acknowledgements

Much of the original research for this book was written within the framework of a project funded by the Swedish Agency for Research Cooperation with Developing Countries. Our first debt of gratitude is therefore clearly with SAREC, for making our collaboration—and this book—possible.

Part of Osvaldo Sunkel's work in this book originated in a paper written for the Third World Foundation, which was discussed at an international conference held in Cartagena, Colombia.

Most of Chapter 10 originates in a paper by Stephany Griffith-Jones, 'Proposals to Manage Debt Problems: Review and Suggestions for Future Research'; written at the request of—and funded by—the Economic and Social Research Council (ESRC).

A number of colleagues at the Institute for Development Studies (IDS) and at the Comisión Económica para America Latina (CEPAL), as well as in other places, have provided us with very useful suggestions and insights on the subject. In particular, we are grateful to the late Dudley Seers, to Frances Stewart, Anatole Kaletsky, Michael Lipton, and Reg Green for valuable discussions. We are also grateful to Surendra Patel and Carlos Fortin, who encouraged us so consistently to write this book, in the midst of so many other activities.

We also wish to thank Danielle Hodges, who so efficiently typed the manuscript, and Susan Frenk, who translated two chapters from Spanish to English.

Stephany Griffith-Jones, IDS, *Brighton, England*
Osvaldo Sunkel, CEPAL, *Santiago de Chile* ·
October, 1985

Contents

List of Tables

Abbreviations

AID	Agency for International Development (usually: USAID)
BIS	Bank for International Settlements
CEPAL	Comisión Económica para América Latina (see ECLAC below)
CFF	Compensatory Financing Facility (IMF)
ECLAC	(formerly ECLA) Economic Commission for Latin America and the Caribbean
EDF	Export Development Fund
EPN	exchange participation note
GAB	General Agreement to Borrow
IDS	Institute for Development Studies
IFC	International Finance Corporation
ILA	International Lending Agency
ILLR	international lenders of last resort
IMF	International Monetary Fund
LDC	less developed country
LIBOR	London Inter-Bank Offer Rate
ODI	Overseas Development Institute (UK government body)
OECD	Organisation for Economic Co-operation and Development
OPEC	Organization of Petroleum Exporting Countries
PSBR	Public Sector Borrowing Requirement

PREALC	Programa Regional del Empleo para América Latina
SAREC	Swedish Agency for Research Cooperation with Developing Countries
SDR	Special Drawing Rights (issued by the IMF)
SELA	Sistema Económico para América Latina
UNCTAD	United Nations Conference on Trade and Development
UNEP	United Nations Environment Programme
UNIDO	United Nations Industrial Development Organization

CHAPTER I

Introduction

In the early 1980s, widespread debt crises erupted simultaneously in most Latin American countries. The focus of attention, particularly in industrial countries and in international financial institutions, and even in some Latin American quarters, has been limited to the debt crises themselves, their short-term management, and the requirement for Latin American economies to adjust so as to assume future debt servicing. This relates to the concern in industrial countries with the negative impact which potential defaults of large developing-country debtors (or continued reschedulings and arrears) may have on their private banks and, more widely, on their economies, and to the hope in Latin America that 'normality' will be restored in a few years. The link between debt problems and the broader difficulties of the existing system of international financial intermediation has been played down in the literature. So too has the fact that the debt crisis is part and parcel of a more profound and longer-term growth and development crisis, both in Latin America and the industrial countries. In our book we will argue that—although separate—the debt and development crises have common origins and causes, and can only be meaningfully overcome by fundamental changes in the policies of the developed countries, in the international financial system, in national development strategies of developing countries, and by a radical solution to the debt problem. Short-term debt management of debt crises and adjustment of national economies, though largely inevitable as an initial response, are becoming increasingly inadequate and untenable in the face of the deep-seated problems which have surfaced so dramatically in the early 1980s, through the debt crisis and the reversal of the previous long-term growth trends of the Latin American economies.

This book will begin by outlining the severity of the current crisis in economic growth and development in Latin America, the magnitude of which is not fully appreciated even in the continent itself, let alone in the industrial countries. It will then turn to the historical background to the current situation. Firstly, it will examine the increasing contradictions (already evident in the early 1970s) of the Latin American development model, many of which were both postponed and accentuated by the vast expansion of private international lending and borrowing that occurred in the seventies.

A main focus of the book will be an examination of the system of international financial intermediation, related to developing countries, as it has evolved since Bretton Woods, with special emphasis on the last decade. It will be argued that the international monetary system established at Bretton Woods—although an important attempt to promote multilateralism in a universal system—had numerous gaps and contradictions. In relation to developing countries, this system did not create mechanisms and institutions which were appropriate and large enough to maintain a supply of net external financial resources to deficit developing countries which was adequate for these countries' growth and development. This gap in the Bretton Woods system and institutions was filled by different economic actors, who perceived at a particular time that their own economic and/or political interests were well served by channelling flows to developing countries. New actors appeared in each of the decades after the Second World War (foreign investors in the 1950s, official aid agencies in the 1960s, and multinational banks in the 1970s) which were willing and able to play a dymanic role in generating financial flows as those flows were perceived by those agents to serve their own interests. One of the most problematic aspects in the 1980s seems to be the lack of such a new actor willing and able to play such a role, while the actors who played such a role in the past (particularly, but not exclusively, the multinational banks) seem unwilling to do so to the same extent.

The sharp decline in new financial flows to Latin America, combined with a dramatic increase in the cost of servicing the debts contracted in previous periods (caused largely by the huge increase in both nominal and real interest rates), has given rise to an absurd and undesirable situation. Since 1982, Latin America has become a large net exporter of financial resources to the industrialized countries, and particularly to the USA. The magnitude of the negative net transfer of financial resources from Latin America, and its implications both for the economies of that continent and for the bargaining position of these countries' governments, has not been fully perceived. Between 1982 and 1984, the magnitude of the negative net transfer of resources has averaged approximately US $27 billion annually, which is equivalent to around 25 per cent of the region's total exports of goods and services. This is in sharp contrast with the situation up to 1981, when Latin America received large net positive transfers of financial resources from abroad, transfers on which the savings and investment structures of these economies had been increasingly reliant. According to even the most optimistic projections, Latin American countries will be required to go on making such massive transfers abroad for several years, with a continuing negative impact on their economies and on the living standards of their people. This situation is becoming increasingly untenable.

The negative transfer of resources has also implied a shift in the bargaining position of creditors and debtors, which has not been fully understood. When net transfers of financial resources flow towards a developing country, the greater bargaining strength lies with the lenders, as it is they who must ultimately decide to make the new loans and transfer the funds; as a result, the lenders can easily impose all types of conditions, particularly to governments desperately in need of foreign exchange. When there are negative financial flows from a debtor developing country, the greater bargaining strength has potentially shifted to the debtor government, as ultimately it must decide to repay and to make the transfer of funds. As a result, the debtor is in this case, in principle, in the position not only to resist the conditions of the lender but, even more fundamentally, to impose his own.

At present, the conventional question asked in international financial circles is whether Latin American governments (and those of other developing countries) will use 'debtor power' to disrupt the international banking system. We believe the key question is, on the contrary, whether debtor developing countries can and will use 'debtor power' to exert effective pressure for changes to be made in the international financial system that would make it stronger, more stable, and more likely to support the development needs of developing countries. We will argue that such changes would—if introduced—not only benefit developing countries' economies, but also the whole international economy, for example, by enhancing the stability of the international banks and stimulating higher growth of world trade.

In Chapter 10, we will review the type of changes which could be introduced in order (*a*) to reduce the burden of the debt overhang, and (*b*) to secure a more stable and adequate system of international financial intermediation in the future, one that would simultaneously reduce risks to the lenders and suit the developmental needs of the debtors. This chapter will include a discussion of measures such as renewed issues of Special Drawing Rights, broadening of semi-automatic official compensatory facilities, and guarantees for private flows.

Though we believe these reforms to be basically beneficial for most of the actors involved, they clearly have costs, which we will try to evaluate. The political feasibility of alternative approaches will also be discussed.

The debt and development crises are not only linked to insufficiencies in the international financial system, and to the sudden deterioration in the international environment that occurred in the early 1980s; they were also clearly partly caused by development strategies excessively reliant on foreign financial resources to sustain them, with consumption and technological patterns too dependent on imported goods. This was particularly so in the case of countries—such as Chile and Argentina—which in the mid-1970s opened up their economies almost completely and indiscriminately to foreign trade and financial flows. More generally, in many Latin American countries, the development strategies and the economic policies pursued led, in the 1970s and early 1980s, to an excessive proportion of the foreign funds being clearly misused in capital flight, imports of luxury goods, and purchases of arms.

The search for a new international financial system must therefore be accompanied by a search for national development strategies and policies which will make more efficient use of foreign inflows for the debtor countries' growth and development than has been the case in recent years, benefiting both the majority of the debtor countries' population as well as the creditors, whose repayment will be guaranteed by more rapid growth.

The book will argue that, as long as international monetary reform and a substantial alleviation of the debt burden is not forthcoming, Latin American governments should focus their energy and attention on the implementation of national and regional recovery and development strategies aimed at full employment, and at equitable and sustained growth for their economies, and should attach far less importance than they have in recent years to 'debt crises management'. In other words, this implies giving top priority to employment and the satisfaction of the fundamental needs of the majority of the population; making the best possible use of existing natural, capital, and human resources; a severe rationing of foreign exchange in order to allocate it strictly to indispensable imported production and wage goods; promoting export and import-substituting activities; promoting internal savings and investment; and, after making sure that international reserves are at an adequate level to respond to emergencies, devoting such foreign exchange as may be left to serve the debt.

CHAPTER 2

Latin America's Worst Socioeconomic Crisis since the Great Depression

Despite a weak recovery of the Latin American economies in 1984, the poor performance of 1985 confirms that the region is still immersed in its worst economic crisis since 1930. GDP per capita in Latin America in 1985 was nearly 9 per cent lower than in 1980, and similar to that attained in 1976. The 1980s promise to become the lost decade in Latin American economic history:

the downward trend of the per capita gross domestic product over the years 1981–1984 attained dramatic proportions in a large number of countries [see Table 2.1]. Thus, during the period in question the per capita product fell by about 25% in Bolivia and almost 22% in El Salvador; it suffered a reduction of approximately 16% in Uruguay, Venezuela and Guatemala; it went down by between 13% and 14% in Peru and Costa Rica; it decreased by 12% in Argentina, Haiti and Honduras; and it fell by 11% in Chile and 9% in Brasil.[1]

The impact of the present crisis on Latin America has been compared, in its depth and extension, with the Great Depression of 1929–32. There is, however, a fundamental difference. Whereas that depression affected primitive and rural societies, this one is taking place in relatively modern, urban societies, characterized by a dense concentration of population, and of economic and sociopolitical activity, in the metropolis. One of its most overwhelming indicators is the magnitude of undisguised urban unemployment which, it must be recalled, occurs in some of the largest urban concentrations in the world. As Table 2.2 shows, urban unemployment increased sharply between 1979 and 1984 in all countries for which data is available. With the exception of Brazil and Mexico, where the increase has been relatively modest, the rate of urban unemployment has doubled in Argentina, Bolivia, Uruguay, and Venezuela, and has grown considerably in Colombia, Costa Rica, Chile, Paraguay, and Peru. These figures may not look particularly striking in view of the large unemployment prevalent in most European economies. But there are at least three fundamental aggravating factors. The first is that the Latin American poor do not have accumulated assets of durable goods. Secondly, there are little or no social security and unemployment benefits to compensate for unemployment. Third, this increase in unemployment is over and above massive rates of urban and rural underemployment.

Another phenomenon which hits the urban population particularly hard, especially the unemployed workers and the marginalized sectors, is inflation.

The rate of inflation gathered enormous speed in Argentina and, above all, in Bolivia, and continued to be very high in Brazil and Peru. The rate of increase of prices also accelerated sharply, although starting from very different levels, in Uruguay, Nicaragua, Jamaica, Paraguay, Costa Rica, Venezuela and the Dominican Republic. In contrast, inflation declined in Mexico, although it was still high both in historical and in internationally comparative terms; it dropped sharply in Ecuador; it remained at the same levels as in the year before in Chile and Colombia, and it was very low in El Salvador, Haiti, Honduras, Barbados and Panama. (See Table 2.3.)

As a result of all this, serious declines have been registered in the real value of wages, which are in many countries lower now than the levels achieved a decade and a half ago. There has also been deterioration—in some cases to an abysmal level—in nutrition, health, and housing conditions, both as a consequence of the phenomena discussed above and because of drastic cuts in basic investment and social expenditure.

The acute tensions and social and political conflicts characteristic of the Latin American scene in recent years should therefore come as no surprise.

The Declaration of Quito, which emanated from the Latin American Economic Summit celebrated there on 9–13 January 1984, states in paragraph five: 'Latin America and the Caribbean are facing the gravest and most profound economic and social crisis of this century, with unique and unprecedented features.' Despite the extreme nature of the crisis, which gave rise to the highest-level regional political reunion to be held in recent years, and the atrocious economic, social, and political costs which it is provoking in almost all Latin American nations, many bureaucrats, businessmen, scholars, and politicians in various parts of Latin America do not yet seem to have fully grasped the dramatic

Table 2.1. Latin America: evolution of per capita Gross Domestic Product[a]

Country	Dollars at 1970 prices				Growth rates						Cumulative rate
	1970	1980	1983	1984[b]	1980	1981	1982	1983	1984[b]		1981–4[b]
Argentina	1,241	1,334	1,166	1,177	-0.9	-7.7	-6.6	1.4	0.9		-11.8
Bolivia	317	382	295	288	-2.1	-3.5	-11.1	-10.0	-2.2		-24.6
Brazil	494	887	798	809	4.8	-3.8	-1.3	-5.3	1.3		-8.9
Colombia	598	824	804	812	1.9	0.1	-1.2	-1.4	1.0		-1.5
Costa Rica	740	974	834	837	-2.1	-4.9	-9.7	-0.3	0.4		-14.1
Cuba[c]	...	...	...	...	-1.9	14.9	2.0	4.6	...		22.6[d]
Chile	958	1,045	895	928	6.2	4.1	-15.7	-2.4	3.6		-11.2
Ecuador	413	723	678	673	1.9	1.0	-1.1	-6.1	-0.7		-6.9
El Salvador	422	433	344	339	-11.3	-10.9	-8.3	-2.9	-1.4		-21.8
Guatemala	448	589	512	497	0.9	-2.1	-6.2	-5.4	-2.8		-15.5
Haiti	90	114	99	100	5.1	-5.2	-4.9	-3.1	0.4		-12.2

Honduras	313	356	318	314	-0.8	-2.3	-5.1	-3.8	-1.4	-12.0
Mexico	978	1,366	1,284	1,280	5.5	5.1	-3.1	-7.7	-0.3	-6.3
Nicaragua	418	337	331	322	6.7	2.0	-4.4	0.5	-2.8	-4.7
Panama	904	1,174	1,214	1,188	10.5	1.9	3.2	-1.8	-2.2	1.1
Paraguay	383	642	612	611	7.9	5.4	-3.9	-5.9	-0.1	-4.8
Peru	659	690	593	598	1.2	1.2	-2.2	-13.2	0.9	-13.3
Dominican Republic	398	601	615	611	3.6	1.6	-0.7	1.5	-0.7	1.7
Uruguay	1,097	1,426	1,226	1,195	5.3	1.2	-10.3	-5.3	-3.5	-16.2
Venezuela	1,239	1,310	1,147	1,097	-5.1	-3.3	-2.2	-7.4	-4.4	-16.2
Total[e]	709	982	893	895	3.1	-0.7	-3.3	-5.3	0.2	-8.9

Source: ECLAC, *Preliminary Overview of the Latin American Economy 1984*, Santiago de Chile.

Notes:

a. At market prices.
b. Provisional estimates subject to revision.
c. Refers to total social product.
d. Refers to 1981–3.
e. Average, excluding Cuba.

Table 2.2. Latin America: evolution of urban unemployment, 1979–84 (Average annual rates)

Country	1979	1980	1981	1982	1983	1984
Argentina[a]	2.0	2.3	4.5	4.8	4.1	4.0
Bolivia[b]	7.6	7.5	9.7	9.4	12.1	13.3
Brazil[c]	6.4	7.2	7.9	6.3	6.7	7.5
Colombia[d]	8.9	9.7	8.2	9.3	11.8	13.5
Costa Rica[e]	5.3	6.0	9.1	9.9	8.5	7.9
Chile[f]	13.4	11.7	9.0	20.0	19.0	18.6
Mexico[g]	5.7	4.5	4.2	4.1	6.9	6.3
Nicaragua[h]	21.4	18.3	15.9	18.5	18.9	19.8
Panama[i]	11.6	9.8	11.8	10.3	11.2	...
Paraguay[j]	5.9	4.1	2.2	5.6	8.4	...
Peru[k]	6.5	7.1	6.8	7.0	9.2	10.9
Uruguay[l]	8.3	7.4	6.7	11.9	15.5	14.5
Venezuela[m]	5.8	6.6	6.8	7.8	10.5	13.9

Source: ECLAC, *Preliminary Overview of the Latin American Economy in 1984.*

Notes:
a. Greater Buenos Aires. Average April–October 1984, April.
b. La Paz 1977, 1978, and 1979, second semester; 1980, average May–October; 1983, second semester; 1984, first semester.
c. Metropolitan areas of Rio de Janeiro, Sao Paulo, Belo Horizonte, Porto Alegre, Salvador, and Recife. Average for 12 months; 1980, average June–December; 1984, average January–October.
d. Bogotá, Barranquilla, Medellín, and Cali. Average for March, June, September, and December; 1984, average for March, June, and September.
e. National urban. Average for March, July, and November; 1984, March.
f. Greater Santiago. Average for four quarters; 1984, average for three quarters. As from August 1983 data relate to the metropolitan area of Santiago.
g. Metropolitan areas of México City, Guadalajara, and Monterrey. Average for four quarters. 1984, average for first two quarters.
h. 1979 to 1981, non-agricultural activities; 1982 to 1984, an estimate.
i. National urban; 1980, urban unemployment recorded in the population census taken in that year; 1981, 1982, and 1983, metropolitan area.
j. Asunción, Fernando de la Mora, Lambaré, and urban areas of Luque and San Lorenzo, annual average; 1981, first semester; 1982, second semester.

Notes to Table 2.2 (*cont.*):

k. Metropolitan Lima. 1970, August–September; 1978, average for July–August; 1979, August–September; 1980, April; 1981, June 1982, 1983 and 1984, official estimate for the whole country.
l. Montevideo. Average for two semesters. 1984, average January–September.
m. National urban. Average for two semesters; 1984, first semester.

implications of the present situation. It would appear, in fact, that a sort of mental inertia persists, supported by the inherently overoptimistic official and financial press, which is still riding the crest of the exceptional period of economic growth of the 1950s and 1960s and the credit boom of the 1970s, which accustomed us to the idea that, according to the slogan of a certain government, 'Today we're doing well, tomorrow even better', under circumstances in which, since 1981 Latin American economies and their populations are actually doing very badly and tomorrow will probably do worse.

The development and external debt policies pursued in previous decades aggravated in these countries their traditional conditions of extreme dependence and vulnerability, in the face of an increasingly unstable international economic system. In these conditions, the international economic crisis led to highly restrictive policies as a response to recession, policies intended to stabilize the balance of payments and keep the economies open. Far from alleviating the crisis in development, these policies further exacerbated it.

In concrete terms, these policies took the form of sharp monetary and financial restrictions and decreased public expenditure, which led to a fall in income and expenditure in the private sector. The contraction in expenditure was most marked in investment, which is more flexible and variable, particularly in the construction sector. This led—as has been remarked—to a large increase in unemployment, underemployment, and marginalization, and a fall in real wages and incomes, especially among the low-paid. It resulted in the suspension of payments for public services (water, sewage, refuse collection, electricity, fuel, telephone, etc.) as well as arrears in rental payments and the servicing of housing debts. Equally, there is a considerable lag in the payment of both state and local taxes and rates.

Table 2.3. Latin America: evolution of consumer prices
(Variations from December to December)

Country	1980	1981	1982	1983	1984
Latin America^a	56.5	56.8	84.5	130.8	175.4
Countries with traditionally high inflation:					
Argentina	61.5	71.7	102.8	156.6	208.0
Bolivia	87.6	131.2	209.7	433.7	675.0^b
Brazil^d	23.9	25.2	296.5	328.5	1 682.3^b
Colombia^e	95.3	91.2	97.9	179.2	194.7^b
Chile	26.5	27.5	24.1	16.5	16.4^b
Mexico	31.2	9.5	20.7	23.6	22.2^b
Peru	29.8	28.7	98.8	80.8	59.2^b
Uruguay	59.7	72.7	72.9	125.1	105.8^b
	42.8	29.4	20.5	51.5	63.8^b
Countries with traditionally moderate inflation:					
Barbados	15.4	14.1	12.6	17.2	17.0
Costa Rica	16.1	12.3	6.9	5.5	3.9^f
Ecuador^h	17.8	65.1	81.7	10.7	15.7^g
El Salvador	14.5	17.9	24.3	52.5	19.1^g
Guatemala	18.6	11.6	13.8	15.5	13.1^g
Guyana	9.1	8.7	−2.0	15.4	…
Haiti^i	8.5	29.1	…	…	…
Honduras	15.3	16.4	6.2	12.2	8.6^j
Jamaica	15.0	9.2	9.4	10.2	6.9^k
	28.6	4.8	7.0	14.5	33.1^l

Nicaragua	24.8	23.2	22.2	32.9	40.0^c
Panama	14.4	4.8	3.7	2.0	1.1^g
Paraguay	8.9	15.0	4.2	14.1	25.4^g
Dominican Republic	4.2	7.4	7.1	9.8	21.2^m
Trinidad and Tobago	16.6	11.6	10.8	15.4	13.4^f
Venezuela	19.6	10.8	7.9	7.0	15.7^g

Source: ECLAC, *Preliminary Overview of the Latin American Economy 1984.*

Notes:

a. Totals for Latin America and partial figures for groups of countries represent average variations by countries, weighted by the population in each year.

b. Variation between November 1984 and November 1983.

c. Variation between September 1984 and September 1983.

d. Up to 1979, figures represent the Consumer Price Index in the city of Rio de Janeiro: from 1980 onwards, the variation in the national total.

e. Up to 1980, figures represent the variation in the Consumer Price Index for manual workers; from 1981 onwards, the variation in the national total, including manual workers and emplyees.

f. Variation between August 1984 and August 1983.

g. Variation between October 1984 and October 1983.

h. Up to 1982, figures represent the variation in the Consumer Price Index in the city of Quito; from 1983 onwards, the national Consumer Price Index, urban area.

i. The series represents the variation between September of the year indicated and September of the preceding year.

j. Variation between June 1984 and June 1983.

k. Variation between March 1984 and March 1983.

l. Variation between July 1984 and July 1983.

m. Variation between May 1984 and May 1983.

All of this enlarges the fiscal deficit, which in turn leads to a reduction in public expenditure—especially in investment and social services, the costs of which are easier to cut than current expenses—principally the salaries of public employees.

We are presented, then, with a real recessionary vicious circle, mainly urban in its manifestations, and concentrated above all in the metropolitan areas, which are those requiring the greatest levels of financial resources in order to function.

The combined effect of the fall in commodity prices, the rise in interest rates, and the abrupt contraction of external financing which took place in 1982 (see Chapter 8), led to drastic recessionary policies of internal adjustment intended to achieve stability in the balance of payments, which had been deeply distorted by the excessive ease with which countries became externally indebted. The combination of the external factors referred to above and the drastic internal adjustment, which was basically translated into a substantial drop in imports, has led in recent years to a shift from the enormous influx of foreign finance which characterized the last five years of the previous decade to a position where Latin America 'exports' or transfers large sums of net resources to the developed world. From 1982 to 1984, these transfers reached around US $80,000 million, which represents approximately 25 per cent of total exports in the region during this period (see Table 2.4, column 3). Nevertheless, the external debt has continued to increase, standing in 1984 at US $360 billion and still growing (see Table 2.5), and the servicing requirements alone represented more than 35 per cent of exports between 1982 and 1984 (see Table 2.6).

One of the reasons for the failure to appreciate the gravity of the situation is the belief that it will soon improve, and that there will be a quick return to the 'normality' of past decades. However, as we hope to demonstrate, a realistic perspective in no way endorses these expectations. The deterioration in the long-term conditions for growth of the industrial economies and of the international economy is such that we cannot hope for a restoration this century of the rates of expansion which prevailed in the post-war decades. Nor are conditions auspicious as regards international trade, investment, and particularly external finance for developing countries. Over all this looms the enormous burden of external debt, whose servicing seriously compromises the possibility of

Table 2.4. Latin America: net financing disposable after payment of profits and interest (US $ billion [US $ 1,000 million])

Year	Net inflow of capital	Net payments of profits and interest	Net disposable financing $(3)=(1)-(2)$	Real net disposable financing^a	Exports of goods and services	Net disposable financing / exports of goods and services^b $(6)=(3)/(5)$
	(1)	(2)	(3)	(4)	(5)	(6)
1973–81^c	21.2	11.0	10.2	15.3	64.4	15.8
1982	19.2	37.6	–18.4	–19.1	101.9	–18.1
1983	4.4	34.5	–30.1	–30.9	100.5	–30.0
1984^d	10.6	37.3	–26.7	–26.7	113.0	–23.6

Source: International Monetary Fund, *Balance of Payments Yearbook* (several issues); and ECLAC estimates, on the basis of official figures.

Notes:

a. Obtained by deflating column 3 by the US wholesale price index, base 1984=100.

b. Percentage. Provisional estimates subject to revision.

c. Annual average, for the period.

d. Provisional estimates subject to revision.

Table 2.5. Latin America: total external debt disbursed
(End-of-year balance in US $ billion)

Country	1978	1979	1980	1981	1982	1983	1984^a
Latin America	150.8	181.9	221.0	275.4^b	315.3^b	340.9^b	360.1^b
Oil-exporting countries	64.3	77.5	92.3	118.9	135.6	145.6	153.4
Bolivia^c	1.7	1.9	2.2	2.4	2.3	3.0	3.2
Ecuador	2.9	3.5	4.6	5.8	6.1	6.6	6.8
Mexico	33.9	39.6	49.3	72.0^d	85.5^d	90.0^d	95.9^d
Peru	9.3	9.3	9.5	9.6	11.0	12.4	13.5
Venezuela^e	16.3	23.0	26.5	29.0	31.0	33.5	34.0
Non-oil-exporting countries	86.5	104.3	128.7	156.4	179.6	195.2	206.7
Argentina	12.4	19.0	27.1	35.6	43.6	45.5	48.0
Brazil^f	52.2	58.9	68.3	78.5	87.5	96.5	101.8
Colombia	4.2	5.1	6.2	7.9	9.4	10.4	10.8
Costa Rica	1.8	2.3	3.1	3.3	3.4	3.8	4.0
Chile^g	6.6	8.4	11.0	15.5	17.1	17.4	18.4
El Salvador	.9	.9	1.1	1.4	1.6	2.0	2.3
Guatemala	.8	.9	1.0	1.4	1.5	1.7	1.9
Haiti^c	.2	.2	.2	.3	.4	.4	.6
Honduras	.9	1.2	1.5	1.7	1.8	2.0	2.2
Nicaragua^c	.9	1.1	1.5	2.1	2.7	3.3	3.9
Panama^c	1.7	2.0	2.2	2.3	2.8	3.2	3.5
Paraguay	.6	.7	.8	.9	1.2	1.4	1.5
Dominican Republic	1.3	1.5	1.8	1.8	1.9	2.5	2.8
Uruguay	1.2	1.6	2.1	3.1	4.2	4.5	4.7

Source: ECLAC on the basis of official information; Brazil and Venezuela: ECLAC, on the basis of data from the Bank for International Settlements.
Notes:
a. Provisional figures.
b. Figures not comparable with those previous to 1982, owing to the inclusion of the Mexican commercial banks' debt.
c. Public debt.
d. Including commercial banks' debt. Estimates on the basis of data supplied by the Secretariat of Finance and Public Credit.
e. Including the public debt plus the non-guaranteed long- and short-term debt with financial institutions reporting to the Bank for International Settlements.

Notes to Table 2.5 (*cont.*):

f. Including the total medium- and long-term debt plus the short-term debt with financial institutions reporting to the Bank for International Settlements.

g. Short-, medium-, and long-term debt, excluding the debt with the IMF and short-term credits for foreign trade operations.

Table 2.6. Latin America: ratio of total interest payments to exports of goods and services[a]

Percentages

Country	1977	1978	1979	1980	1981	1982	1983	1984[b]
Latin America	12.4	15.5	17.4	19.9	26.4	39.0	35.8	35.0
Oil-exporting countries	13.0	16.0	15.7	16.5	22.3	32.0	31.0	33.0
Bolivia	9.9	13.7	18.1	24.5	35.5	43.6	49.3	57.0
Ecuador	4.8	10.3	13.6	18.2	24.3	30.1	26.0	31.5
Mexico	25.4	24.0	24.8	23.1	28.7	39.9	36.7	36.5
Peru	17.9	21.2	14.7	16.0	21.8	24.7	31.2	35.5
Venezuela	4.0	7.2	6.9	8.1	12.7	21.0	20.3	25.0
Non-oil-exporting countries	11.9	15.1	18.8	23.3	31.3	46.6	40.7	36.5
Argentina	7.6	9.6	12.8	22.0	31.7	54.6	58.4	52.0
Brazil	18.9	24.5	31.5	34.1	40.4	57.1	43.4	36.5
Colombia	7.4	7.7	10.1	13.3	21.6	25.0	21.7	21.5
Costa Rica	7.1	9.9	12.8	18.0	25.5	33.4	41.8	32.0
Chile	13.7	17.0	16.5	19.3	34.6	49.5	39.4	45.5
El Salvador	2.9	5.1	5.3	6.5	7.5	11.9	14.2	15.0
Guatemala	2.4	3.6	3.1	5.3	7.5	7.8	7.6	4.0
Haiti	2.3	2.8	3.3	2.0	3.2	2.4	4.9	5.0
Honduras	7.2	8.2	8.6	10.6	14.5	22.4	17.7	19.0
Nicaragua	7.0	9.3	9.7	15.7	15.5	33.2	19.3	18.5
Paraguay	6.7	8.5	10.7	14.3	15.9	14.9	24.3	19.0
Dominican Republic	8.8	14.0	14.4	14.7	10.5	22.6	24.9	23.5
Uruguay	9.8	10.4	9.0	11.0	13.1	22.4	27.6	31.5

Source: 1977–83: International Monetary Fund, *Balance of Payments Yearbook*; 1984: ECLAC, on the basis of official data.
Notes:
a. Interest payments include those on the short-term debt.
b. Provisional estimates subject to revision.

even minimal growth in these economies. The most optimistic projections scarcely permit us to envisage the restoration of pre-crisis levels of economic activity until the end of the decade!

To understand further the severity of the current crisis, it is important to bear in mind that it is the culmination of several decades of exceptionally favourable economic growth, an abundance of external and internal financial resources, both public and private, and high investment and expenditure, especially in urban areas and above all in the metropolis. What hopes may we hold for the future, then, when the problems of unemployment, poverty, and inequality, particularly in the cities, will become more acute and the crisis will deepen, under circumstances when public and private resources, both internal and external, will most probably be maintained at approximately their present low levels, without much prospect of an increase and with the possibility of further reductions?

Note

1. Enrique Iglesias, *Preliminary Overview of the Latin American Economy During 1984* ECLAC, LC/G.1336, Santiago de Chile, January 1985. All the information in this chapter, and a number of paragraphs quoted verbatim, are taken from this source.

CHAPTER 3

The Increasing Limitations of the Import Substitution Model towards 1970[1]

The economic crisis which was unleashed in August 1982, when Mexico suspended the servicing of its foreign debt, and the subsequent contraction in the flow of foreign finance to Latin America, has both immediate and conjunctural as well as more distant and structural precedents. We will discuss the more conjunctural factors in Chapter 8.

Among the more long-term, structural factors, we must remind ourselves that the growing external debt, which attained explosive proportions in the final years of the decade, first manifested itself in the decade of the 1960s and was accentuated throughout the following decade. It is linked to four major phenomena which cannot be neglected in a long-term perspective:

(a) the tendency in Latin America towards exhaustion of the process of industrialization through import substitution, which began to prevail towards the end of the 1960s;[2]
(b) the oil crisis of 1973 and the consequent substantial increases in the relative price of oil;
(c) the limitations and general characteristics of the public international financial system;
(d) the reconstitution and rapid expansion of a new international private financial market from the mid-1960s.

As we will argue in the following chapters, this last phenomenon generated a great permissiveness in international private finance in the 1970s—in contrast to previous decades, when external savings were extremely scarce and highly selective, and took the form of public external finance and direct private investment. The enormous expansion of international private finance made it possible to overlook throughout the 1970s the structural and energy crises in which the post-war style of growth had resulted, not only in Latin America but even in the industrialized nations.

The massive expansion in international finance in the 1970s

enabled a large increase in global demand through the recycling of petrodollars to finance countries with considerable balance of payments deficits, incurred by the rise in oil prices. This compensated for the tendency towards stagnation in both the industrialized nations and those in the process of industrializing through import substitution. The huge scale of exports to the OPEC nations and the maintenance of import levels by countries with external difficulties deriving from the process of import substitution or the rise in oil prices, or both, were important factors in maintaining external demand for the industrialized nations, at a time when these countries were adopting restrictive internal policies which exacerbated structural tendencies towards stagnation.

In those countries whose processes of import substitution were already becoming exhausted, whether they were net importers or exporters of oil, the easy access to international finance allowed the former to attenuate growing external restrictions through external borrowing, and the latter to increase imports well beyond the new high level which the price of oil made possible. It also led them to get into debt, especially later on, when the relative prices of oil began to deteriorate while the disproportionate investment programmes and uncontrolled expansion in consumption and arms acquisition continued apace.

The origins and expansion of the external debt (although not its explosive growth in the past few years) are structurally rooted in the tendency towards exhaustion of the import substitution model of industrialization which began to prevail towards the end of the 1960s, reflected especially in the marked and increasing external disequilibria. The recourse to private external finance and the consequent external indebtedness, hand in hand with the continued —albeit irregular—expansion of the international economy during the 1970s, prolonged and alleviated the agony of the import substitution model. An important role was played in the process (more in some countries than in others) by attempts to attenuate the external constraint and the limitations of the internal market by diversifying into exports of manufactured goods and other non-traditional exports, a task that was not made easy in a world of highly protected markets.

The prospects for the future, as we shall see later, are scarce net foreign finance, limited growth in the industrial economies, and difficult access to the markets of the industrialized nations. Consequently, the Latin American nations will now inevitably be obliged to confront the structural crisis of their growth, which was already present around 1970 but which they were able to postpone thanks to the particular circumstances prevailing at the time. This is the fundamental reason, apart from social and political considerations, why policies of short-term adjustment have no future. They presuppose a return to a certain normality following the adjustment, but such expectations are fallacious. Successive adjustments, particularly in the face of new international conditions, will lead, not to 'normality', but to a renewed encounter with a deep structural crisis, dating from many years, aggravated by policies which tried to avoid it for a decade and a half. This is why the theme of development strategies for future growth will soon be back on the agenda. We will return to this theme in the final chapter of the book.

Some key aspects of the crisis in the import substitution process refer to the fact that this stage of industrialization failed to produce the expected results. In particular, it did not fulfil one of the basic objectives attributed to it: to overcome foreign dependence. This would have required a substantial expansion of manufacturing exports. But that option was simply not open to the newly industrializing countries of the 1930s, 1940s, and 1950s. At that period in history, during their initial stages of industrialization, the international economic and financial system had completely broken down as a consequence of the Great Depression, a situation prolonged during and after the Second World War, characterized by highly protected markets and profound disequilibria in the international trade, investment, finance, and exchange markets. The international environment was decidedly unfavourable to Latin American industrialization, with regard not only to the possibilities for exporting manufactures, but even to the industrialization policies themselves. Faced with protected external markets, very limited availability of hard foreign currency, and extremely scarce and ideologically hostile external financial sources, the industrialization process had nowhere to turn but inward, in the direction of the import substitution process.

Even if this type of industrialization permitted the reduction of the proportion of the value of imports in relation to GNP—the import coefficient—it also effected an extremely important change in the structure of imports. If, several decades ago, a large proportion of available foreign exchange was devoted to purchasing non-essential consumer goods, towards 1970—at least in the most industrialized economies of the region—imports were restricted almost exclusively to essential goods: machinery, equipment, and tools to maintain and expand productive capacity; raw materials and intermediate products to ensure a normal level of economic activity; and even, quite frequently, basic foodstuffs to maintain popular consumption. That is to say, the Latin American and Caribbean economies arrived at a situation of extreme external vulnerability, where any alteration in external prices or the slightest problem of foreign financing would cause serious difficulties, such as shortage and rising prices of essential consumer goods, the restriction of imports of raw materials and the consequent effect on the development of manufacturing activity, or the effect on productive capacity of delaying imports of machinery and equipment.

This paradoxical result—greater industrialization plus greater vulnerability and dependence—was to a large extent a consequence of the way in which the policy of industrialization was carried out in Latin America: the so-called 'import substitution process'. In situations in which foreign exchange became insufficient, the importation of consumer durables was limited. But, since the internal demand for these goods was not reduced, while the importation of the machinery and goods necessary to produce them was favoured, conditions were created which made it possible to produce such goods in the country. While protection was meant to favour national industry, multinational enterprises also took advantage and, in a sort of acrobatic leap, overcame the protectionist tariffs and the policies of prohibition of imports of finished goods, and installed themselves within the Latin American nations. In this way, goods which had previously been imported began to be produced domestically; but, in order to do this, it was necessary not only to import the requisite equipment and machinery as well as a considerable proportion of the components for the finished manufacture, but also to incur financial costs in foreign exchange which eventually came to constitute an overwhelming burden in many countries. This was due not only to the fact that a large part of this industry was foreign-owned—subsidiaries of large multinational companies—and that many products were manufactured under licence or technical assistance contracts which were paid for in various ways, but also to the fact that public and private financing from abroad was necessary in order to accelerate industrialization and investment in infrastructure. Thus the process of import substitution resulted, on the one hand, in great balance of payments vulnerability and, on the other, in foreign financial commitments which in some Latin American countries came to represent a considerable proportion of current foreign exchange receipts.

It was this situation which forced these countries to recognize that one of the most important objectives of industrialization was the increase and diversification of exports, not just because of the well-known instability which results from dependence on a single export product, but also because the process of import substitution had led to a rigid import structure through what Prebisch has called 'the elimination of the margin of imports.'[3] That is to say, with such a limited availability of foreign exchange, after deducting the servicing of foreign financial commitments, only the importation of production goods and essential consumer goods was possible. Accordingly, should an unfavourable situation arise in foreign markets or in export production, the only alternatives were the contraction of essential consumption and economic activity, or additional foreign indebtedness.

On the other hand—and this is of the utmost importance—as the importation of production goods came to represent a high and ever-growing proportion of total imports, the traditional export activities were transformed, *de facto*, into capital goods industries. The increase of exports, therefore, whether agricultural, fishing, mining, or manufacturing, consequently came to be the equivalent of an expansion in real national saving and investment capacity, the essential prerequisite for development. The rapid increase of exports thus opened up the possibility of basing growth progressively on national savings or—which amounts to the same thing—on nationally owned industry. Conversely, the stagnation of exports, if the rhythm of growth was to be maintained, demanded greater foreign savings and investment, with the resulting additional indebtedness. But this implied an increasing denationalization of national wealth, either of the actual ownership of industries when the savings were brought in as foreign private capital, or as a financial claim on the wealth of the nation as a whole, when the foreign savings took the form of loans. This was the main option taken up in the 1970s as the international private financial market expanded.

In countries without a sufficiently developed national capital goods industry and with a rigid import structure, any possibility of national development depends on the expansion of exports. In fact, this was the root of the central failing of the import substitution policy: the importation of capital and intermediary goods necessary to produce consumer goods was substituted for the importation of the consumer goods themselves. A structure of manufacturing production was created which was geared principally to producing for the consumer, while the traditional export sector, along with some diversification into manufactures and non-traditional exports, and above all the foreign debt, were left to 'produce' the investment goods. This is the fundamental reason why the development process became structurally increasingly dependent, vulnerable, and unstable.

Another of the characteristic features inherited from this stage of industrialization was the establishment of a very large and active state. Based increasingly on the appropriation of a considerable part of the financial resources of export activity, which by virtue of its high productivity was the only sector of the economy capable of generating an abundant surplus of taxable income, the state came to fulfil three new principal functions: (*a*) as a financial intermediary, to transfer financial resources and subsidize the development of private industry, usually by means of specialized development institutions; (*b*) as a mechanism for income redistribution, allocating resources to the expansion of social security and to the extension of educational, housing, and health services; and (*c*) as a mechanism of public investment, adapting and enlarging the economic infrastructure in transportation, communications, and power, as well as some basic industrial enterprises. As can be appreciated, the process of industrialization and development begun in the decade of the 1930s in what are now the most industrialized countries of Latin America, and more recently in the other Latin American countries, depended on the fundamental support of the public sector. The state has fulfilled two strategic functions in development policy: the appropriation of resources in the highly productive export activities, on the one hand, and their reassignment in order to promote industrial and social development on the other.

In this new function, the state confronted two contrary tendencies which were becoming increasingly acute. On the one hand, there was an insatiable thirst for appropriating resources in order to use them in programmes of industrialization and infrastructure, especially in the area of social services. On the other hand, the goose which laid the golden eggs—the export sector—had remained relatively stagnant, due to policies and economic and technological trends whose origin lay in the world's developed industrialized economies, over which Latin American countries have had little influence. Consequently, once the principal base of the taxation system stagnated and tax rates reached a certain level, revenues no longer grew at a rhythm commensurate with the rapidly increasing needs of the public sector. The political and administrative problems of quickly and efficiently extending the taxation system to the rest of the economy, and the problems derived from the characteristics of the economic structure itself, thus determined a systematic and permanent tendency towards deficit in the public sector. Moreover, given the instability of the income derived from the export sector, the deficit became more acute when foreign markets were depressed, and lessened in more prosperous periods, while the new functions acquired by the state entailed new permanent financial commitments which had a dynamic of their own.

As a result of the stagnation of traditional agriculture, the structure of foreign trade, the type of industrialization, and the function fulfilled by the state, these countries became—from the point of view of the structure and functioning of the economy— entirely dependent on their foreign economic relations. The most serious aspect of this is that this extreme dependence was rooted in the vulnerability and structural deficit of the balance of payments, in the fact that the type of industrialization and the form of exploitation of the export sector have not permitted Latin American and Caribbean countries—with a few exceptions—to acquire the capacity for the adaptation and creation of technology, and in the fact that an important and probably growing part of industry and of export activities are either foreign-owned or depend on licences and foreign technical assistance. All these factors weigh heavily on the availability of foreign exchange, and on the fact that both the fiscal sector and the balance of payments persistently tend towards deficit—except on very exceptional occasions—leading to the necessity of foreign financing. In certain conditions, this foreign financing can entail the accumulation of such considerable debt that the very servicing of the debt requires resort to additional foreign financing—a genuine vicious circle. It is this aspect—the overwhelming and implacable necessity to obtain foreign financing—which encapsulates the situation of dependence; this is the crucial point in the mechanism of dependence, as has been amply and tragically demonstrated in the past few years.

During the 1970s, the crisis in the import substitution model of industrialization gave rise to increasingly acute economic difficulties and instabilities, with serious social and political repercussions. These led to a series of modifications in development strategies and policies, ranging from changes of emphasis to radical reorientations, which may be grouped in three general categories.

On the one hand, certain countries persisted with the policies that they had previously pursued, although making some important corrections, especially in the strong emphasis they placed on promoting manufactures and other non-traditional exports (as was the case with, for example, Brazil, Colombia, and Mexico). The other two alternatives constituted much more radical changes, of a totally different nature.

One tendency followed a pronounced socializing, statist, re-distributive line, as in the attempts at transition to socialism, or towards more socialized economies, in Chile, Peru, Argentina, and Jamaica. The other, in complete contrast, took a frankly monetarist and neo-liberal track, opening the economy to foreign capital, relegating the state to a subsidiary role, and reaffirming the role of the market-place and of national and international private industry. This tendency, which succeeded attempts at socialism in Chile, Peru, and Argentina, spread—in the radical form which characterized the entire Southern Cone—to Uruguay, and had important expressions in other countries, such as Costa Rica and Venezuela.

For different reasons, all these attempts failed, and, rather than contributing to a solution, further aggravated the crisis in the import substitution model which had been unleashed towards the end of the 1960s. This is the backcloth against which we should now discuss the themes of adjustment, revival, and new strategies for development, more than a decade and a half since they were first mooted.

The origins and evolution of the import substitution strategy are undoubtedly, to a large extent, the consequence of the internal policies followed by the countries in question, particularly as regards its persistence in some countries towards the 1960s. But, as mentioned before, they were partly caused by, and also conditioned by a highly constrained international environment, product of the breakdown of the international economic system at the time of the Great Depression and, later, by the disruption in the international economy caused by the Second World War. The post-war (Bretton Woods) new international financial system was not geared to the development needs of the industrializing countries. We will examine some of the contributions and deficiencies of this post-war situation and its evolution in the next three chapters.

Notes

1. This chapter draws heavily on an article published by one of the authors almost two decades ago, and which, to our surprise, seems as relevant today as when it was written. See Osvaldo Sunkel, 'National Development Policy and External Dependence in Latin America', *Journal of Development Studies*, October 1969 (first published in Spanish, *Estudios Internacionales*, April 1967).
2. There is a large bibliography on the crisis and exhaustion of the import substitution model. It is worth bearing in mind that the critique of this process is one of the principal origins of the theme of dependency.
3. Raúl Prebisch, 'Desarrollo Económico o Estabilidad Monetaria: El Falso Dilema', CEPAL, *Boletin Económico de América Latina*, March 1961.

CHAPTER 4

The Bretton Woods International Financial System: Its Contribution and Its Contradictions

A brief theoretical interlude

One of the key issues facing the international economy, at the level both of theory and of practice, is related to appropriate levels and mechanisms for international financial intermediation. The essence of the problem has been discussed for a long time in economic theory; however, the problem became significantly more acute in the 1970s, as both current account deficits and surpluses, particularly of different categories of developing countries, rocketed. Furthermore, the issues have become somewhat more complex as financial intermediation internationally has acquired new and more complicated facets, alongside the still fundamental, classical purpose of channelling savings into productive investment. As the superstructure of investments and currencies has become enormous and complex, as the world's needs have become more differentiated, the result has been that many more of the gross flows through the capital markets of the world today reflect financial decisions that are not directly tied (and which do not necessarily lead) to physical capital formation.

The problem of financial intermediation arises, at the national and at the international level, mainly because those economic agents which save are not the same ones which invest. Both nationally and internationally, if financial intermediation between net savers and net investors is not performed adequately, the effect will be to depress the level of output and income to the point at which the excess of savings is eliminated.

As Keynes pointed out,[1] at a national level it will always be true that *ex post* savings will equal *ex post* investment; similarly, at an international level, *ex post* the sums of individual countries' balance of payments deficits and surpluses must always add to zero, and *ex post* balance of payments surpluses and deficits will have been financed (even though recently the mechanisms of finance have taken such unorthodox forms as voluntary and involuntary arrears on debt servicing and payment on imports). The key issue in the international economy—following the parallel with the national economy—is *not* so much that the financing of surpluses and deficits has taken place and will take place in an *ex post* sense, but rather what *levels* of deficits are sustainable by the financing process, and what *level* of economic activity in the deficit countries and in the world economy can be sustained.

The level of economic activity is not only determined by the amount and distribution of financial intermediation but also by the form of national adjustment to current account surpluses and deficits undertaken by individual countries. In particular, we will focus here on the much-neglected issue of adjustment by surplus countries, as the level of those countries' economic activity will influence the necessary financial flows required to sustain a particular level of economic activity in countries with current account deficits.

As is well known, Keynes attributed the existence of income levels which imply high levels of unemployment of the labour force and spare capacity, in a national context, mainly to lack of effective demand. What is less known is that he extended this analysis to the international context. Thus, in 1942[2] he wrote the following—which seems particularly relevant again in the 1980s:

If, indeed, a country lacks the productive capacity to maintain its standard of life, then a reduction in this standard is not avoidable. If its wage and price levels in terms of money are out of line with those elsewhere, a change in the rate of its foreign exchange is inevitable. But if, possessing the productive capacity, it lacks markets because of restrictive policies throughout the world, then the remedy lies in expanding its opportunities for export by removal of the restrictive pressures. We are too ready today to assume the inevitability of unbalanced trade positions. It used to be supposed, without sufficient reason, that effective demand is always properly adjusted throughout the world; we now tend to assume, equally without sufficient reason, that it never can be. On the contrary, there is great force in the contention that, if active employment and ample purchasing power can be sustained in the main centers of world trade, the problem of surpluses and unwanted exports will largely disappear, even though, under the most prosperous conditions, there may remain disturbances of trade and unforeseen situations requiring special remedies.

Keynes's proposals at Bretton Woods

After this analysis, Keynes follows on with his main policy proposal:

There is no obvious means of offering a right measure of inducement to the general expansion of international trade except by a broadly based international organization . . . the International Clearing Union.

Such a Clearing Union (whose main characteristics will be briefly described below) would have explicit and clear analogies with the development of the history of credit money at the national level, where the banking system eliminated hoarding by centralizing savings and 'recycling' them to investors, with positive results for all:

Just as the development of national banking systems served to offset a deflationary pressure which would have prevented otherwise the development of modern industry, so by extending the same principle to the international field we may hope to offset the contractionist pressure which might otherwise overwhelm in social disorder and disappointment the good hopes of our modern world. The substitution of a credit mechanism for hoarding would have repeated in the international field the turning of stone into bread.[3]

The main characteristics of the international bank which Keynes proposed[4] were the following:

1. The bank (which he called Clearing Union) would have organized a multilateral clearing of the bilateral imbalances between central banks, through which all international payments would have been centralized and directed.

2. The operations of the Clearing Union would have been carried out in a new international reserve asset, which he called 'bancor'.

3. Member countries would have been able to build up credit balances or draw on overdraft facilities with the Clearing Union. Interest would have been charged both on overdraft facilities *and on excessive credit bancor holdings*; this latter proposal had the explicit aim to encourage *also* the adjustment of surplus countries, thus introducing a far greater symmetry to adjustment than then existed, and also reducing the deflationary bias to the world economy which an emphasis only on adjustment of deficit countries implied (and, incidentally, still implies).

4. Keynes's proposal implied a very large institution, which would allow unconditional access to large overdraft rights of at least US $26 billion, in which the potential US liability could have amounted to as much as US $23 billion.[5] To perceive the importance of this sum, in present terms, it seems interesting that, according to Williamson's recent calculations,[6] this would be equivalent in 1983 to a one-off SDR allocation of over SDR 720 billion, with no acceptance limit!

The US position in the debates before—and at—Bretton Woods were significantly different to those of Keynes and the British delegation; the US Government's main aim was to create a fund that would 'maintain international equilibrium at a high level of international trade', and therefore to secure from members 'commercial policies designed to reduce trade barriers and to terminate discriminatory practices'.

The system created at Bretton Woods

As is well known, in almost every case where the initial view of the US Government differed from those of the British, the Articles of the International Monetary Fund ultimately reflected the former proposal—which was inevitable, given the relative financial, economic, and political muscle of the USA and Britain at the time. Thus, the post-war order established at Bretton Woods implied:

(*a*) the restriction of competitive exchange markets

(*b*) perpetuation of the gold exchange standard, without creation of any new international reserve asset (until 1970, when Special Drawing Rights were created).

(*c*) no effective adjustment pressures on surplus countries; the US delegation introduced a 'scarce currency clause', as a concession to the UK and other deficit countries, which allowed members to limit 'the freedom of exchange operations' in the currencies of a country with a large surplus; this amendment, which reflected partly a technical concern that the Fund might otherwise have been placed in the position of promising to provide a currency that it did not have, was also interpreted as a desire to meet British wishes for a guarantee or symmetry in adjustment pressures exercised by the Fund. However, in the event, the scarce currency clause was *never* applied, and so no effective direct pressure has ever been applied by the International Monetary Fund on surplus countries.

(*d*) perhaps most important of all, creation of *a Fund which was significantly smaller than that envisaged by Keynes*. The size of the Fund created was US $8.8 billion, with a US contribution of US $3.2 billion (as opposed to a minimum of US $26 billion and US $23 billion proposed in the Keynes Plan—see above). Although it was deliberately not made clear at the time, the US position was that lending by the IMF, except on a very limited scale, should imply stringent conditions on the borrowing countries' policies. As has been clearly described by Dell (1981),[7] conditionality was not explicitly introduced in the initial IMF Articles of Agreement ratified at Bretton Woods, but was later introduced, as other countries gave in to US Government views.

Doubtless the Bretton Woods system (and the institutions it created, the IMF and the World Bank) implied a bold attempt at promoting multilateralism in a universal system with clear rules, which helped to avoid many of the serious economic difficulties of the inter-war years. As such, it contributed to post-war reconstruction, and to the remarkable period of growth of world production and trade in the 1950s and 1960s; the international co-operation it achieved was significantly in advance of anything achieved in earlier periods.

From another angle, the setting up of the IMF and the World Bank can be seen as major steps in the growth of a public international financial system, to a large extent set up to replace the private international financial system which had practically disappeared after the 1930s *débâcle*. This new public international system also included national state agencies responsible for extending or guaranteeing export credits (of which Eximbank, the Export–Import Bank of the USA, was a forerunner), and later additions, such as the regional development banks (of which the Inter-American Development Bank was the first to be created); a range of public bilateral and multilateral aid institutions (such as AID) were also set up during the 1950s and early 1960s. A complex and new set of public international financial institutions thus developed, implying an important step forward in regulated public international financial intermediation. However, as we will see below, the system which emerged was on a scale too reduced to make an adequate contribution to external development finance in the 1950s and 1960s; in the 1970s, the dramatically increased size of the problem of financing developing countries' deficits, and the limited response of the public international financial system, implied that the public system was able to make only a relatively marginal contribution to deficit countries' funding.

Thus, in spite of the contribution of the Bretton Woods system to post-war growth, the gaps and weaknesses in it led eventually to increasing contradictions, which implied the breakdown of the system in some of its specific aspects, and the curtailment of its contribution to the growth of world output and trade. It would seem that Keynes's theoretical and institutional vision would have implied a far more significant advance in the level of organization of the international financial system, and would have helped to avoid many of the contradictions which emerged in the Bretton Woods system; it is noteworthy in this respect that major attempts at reforming or even replacing the Bretton Woods system (for example, the Triffin Plan, the US Government proposals for reform in the early 1970s, the proposals in the Brandt Commission reports) use elements which are similar (or are based on similar principles) to those contained in the original Keynes Plan; in particular, the need for a far greater role for an international currency, larger public international financial institutions, and some effective measures of exerting pressure on countries with current account surpluses.

Naturally, not all—perhaps not even most—of Keynes's detailed proposals for an International Clearing Union would be relevant today, in a significantly different world to that of the mid-1940s. Similarly, many of the contradictions which emerged in the Bretton Woods system were due not only to the original limitations of, and gaps in, this system, but to its relative slowness in adpating to rapid economic and political changes. Amongst these changes are (*a*) increasing international interdependence (which makes individual national economies far more vulnerable to developments in other parts of the world economy, in areas such as large private capital movements across borders and increased synchronization of business cycles amongst different countries), and (*b*) an increased number of countries—and a significant growth in the number of developing countries—who are now major actors in global issues; this had led to a world economy with a multi-polar character, in sharp contrast to the immediate post-war period, when the US economy's importance was far greater than it is now.

In the preceding discussion we have highlighted Keynes's contribution to the debates on the post-war order in the field of international economic and financial relations. We have done so for two reasons; first, as pointed out, such a theoretical perception at an international level would have seemed to assure higher levels of world trade, output, and employment, and a more rational international economic organization. Secondly, Keynes was concerned with protecting the interests of countries which—like his own, the UK, and most of Europe—would emerge from the Second World War with significant current account deficits, and in need of restoring or reconstructing their economy.[8] Many of those concerns ceased to be so relevant to those countries after their economies recovered—and, in several cases, even had current account surpluses for long periods; those concerns were, and still are, extremely relevant to the interests of developing countries, who by the very nature of their low incomes, and by their wish to achieve growth and development, tend to have structural deficits in their balance of payments, as explained in Chapter 3.

Most authors agree that the economic development process normally includes a requirement both for long-term external capital and for short-term balance of payments assistance to finance both long-term and short-term current account deficits of developing countries; furthermore, most countries which are now industrialized (and particularly the USA, Canada, Australia, and New Zealand) relied heavily on foreign capital and foreign lending for their development.[9]

There is little consensus amongst economic theorists and development practitioners about the *exact* relationship between external capital and development, even though it is generally accepted that external capital is necessary for accelerating development. In Latin America, amongst those critical of the role of external capital because of its potentially negative effects on national autonomy have been analysts, linked to the *dependencia* school. For example, Sunkel wrote in 1969: 'it is in this aspect . . . the overbearing and implacable necessity to obtain external financing . . . which finally sums up the situation of dependency; this is the crucial mechanism of dependency.'[10] The need for development finance is, however, not denied by those critical of some of its negative effects.

An important contribution towards clarifying the link between external capital and development was made by Raul Prebisch, whose thinking on these—as well as on other matters—has been very influential, both world-wide and in Latin America in particular.

In his many writings and reports, Prebisch (for example in 1959, 1964, and 1979;[11] pointed out that acceleration of the rate of growth of developing countries implies more than a proportionate increase in the demand for imports, as a tendency to external disequilibrium is inherent in the process of development. Prebisch emphasized, particularly in his earlier writings, that developing countries faced deteriorating 'terms of trade', as the lower growth of demand for primary products, by comparison with that relating to industrial products, meant that developing countries' export prices expanded less than that of the industrial goods which they required; to overcome this problem, developing countries embarked on a process of industrialization—which, however, accelerated demand for imports of manufactured and other goods, creating a serious bottleneck that, if not overcome, may inhibit development.

Together with other measures, taken both at a national and an international level, a transfer of foreign financial resources can play, according to Prebisch, an important role in helping to eliminate or control these financial disequilibria. Prebisch stressed in his writings[12] that several conditions need to be met for such flows to contribute to development: (a) the net volume of foreign flows must be appropriate to development needs; (b) the outflows generated for payments of profits and interests must still allow for future net flows; it is therefore desirable that the financial terms of such flows (in relation to maturities, grace period, and level of interest rate) are not too onerous; and (c) the net external financial flows are used for investments which will contribute to an increase in exports and/or a substitution of exports.

Prebisch, and other analysts in the ECLA tradition, have also stressed that net foreign financial flows towards third world countries will make a positive contribution towards those countries' development, if such flows are accompanied by other measures, both nationally and internationally. At a national level, Prebisch emphasizes measures that will improve income distribution and which will broaden markets for industrial development; internationally, he has stressed, for example, measures which will give access to exports of industrial products from developing countries, both in industrial countries and in other developing countries.

As we saw above, the proposal which preceded the creation of the Bretton Woods institution (in particular Keynes's proposals discussed above) implied that the channelling of such flows to developing countries would have been carried out to an important extent through a central public international financial institution. As we have already discussed briefly above, and will examine in much more detail below, the net contribution of the Bretton Woods institutions to the financing of the large developing countries' current account deficits has *de facto* been relatively limited; this limited contribution was particularly evident in the 1970s, when those deficits increased so dramatically.

As the needs for financing current account deficits of developing countries were covered only to such a small extent by the Bretton Woods institutions, and as different economic and/or political agents perceived the channelling of financial flows to third world countries as a measure which would serve their own interests well, such agents *de facto* played a major or dominant role in providing foreign exchange to developing countries in general, and to Latin America in particular. In the 1950s it was the foreign investors pursuing greater profits who provided the main source of finance. During the 1960s, official aid agencies—largely of a bilateral type—played the most dynamic role, as aid was perceived in this decade to be in the interests of industrial countries' governments, and particularly in the interests of the USA. During the 1970s, the most dynamic actors were the multinational banks, which rapidly expanded their lending to several Latin American countries in search of greater profits. As we shall discuss in more detail below, one of the most problematic aspects in the world economy of the 1980s seems to be the lack of a new actor, willing and able to play a dynamic role in the financing of the Third World in general, and of Latin America in particular. At the same time, the actors who played a dynamic role in former decades (for example, multinational banks and official aid agencies) are very unwilling to continue to do so to the same extent in the future.

In each decade, after the Second World War, the flows were initiated mainly by institutions or enterprises based in the USA, and then the process became 'internationalized' as institutions or enterprises from other countries increased their share in these flows; flows originating from US institutions tended, however, to play a major role throughout. The financing of these large capital exports from the USA were, particularly in the 1970s, not based mainly on a US current account surplus or a decline in US foreign exchange reserves, but were financed by a large increase in holding of US dollars by foreign official institutions. US multinational companies, aid agencies, and multinational banks were basically able to make such financial transfer because the rest of the world was (and is) willing to accept the dollar as an international means of payment and store of value.

Thus, different agents have *de facto* provided external finance to developing countries, and to Latin America in particular, when they perceived that this suited their interests. However, when the channelling of new flows were perceived as no longer suiting these agents' interests, (due to changes either in the developing countries or in the world economy), such new flows were, naturally, significantly reduced. As a result of such changes, net flows, or net lending to those countries (defined as disbursements minus principal repayments), decline significantly; net transfers (which measure net flows minus interest and profit remittances) *may become negative*, with harmful effects for these countries. In fact, this occurred in Latin America in the early 1980s; *for the 1982–4 period, the total negative net transfer represented a reduction in import capacity equivalent to approximately 25 per cent of exports of goods and services.*[13]

As we shall see below, (particularly in Chapter 8) this dramatic change in net transfer is not only due to changed attitudes by lenders and investors, but is also influenced by changes in the international economy, such as an increase in interest rates, combined with a relative reduction of developing countries' export prices. Furthermore, particularly in the case of international commercial credit, net flows have often been pro-cyclical, that is, increasing when a country's balance of payments showed a relative improvement, or when its prospects improved, and declining (or even becoming negative) when a country's balance of payments situation deteriorated; it is for this that the private banks have been called 'fair weather friends'.

Because financial flows to Latin America did not correspond to

38   *The Bretton Woods System*

a mechanism deliberately designed to suit the countries' and the world economy's needs, but were instead basically dependent on the changing perceived interests of the agents generating such flows, they tended not to be sustained at a level consistent with the financing requirements of developing countries. In fact, during the 1960s and 1970s new flows—generated by the new dynamic actors, official aid agencies in the 1960s and multinational banks in the 1970s—helped service the outflows corresponding to the actor which had played a dynamic role in the previous decade. This was particularly significant in the 1960s, when new inflows of aid to Latin America (see Chapter 5) could be said basically to have coincided in magnitude with net outflows to foreign direct investors. The problem of servicing past loans became much more severe when a large proportion of credit was contracted by developing countries at floating interest rates in the 1970s; this made the level of servicing of those debts highly dependent on economic policy abroad (in particular that of the USA). Price instability, which had long been a feature of commodity trade, therefore became characteristic of the transfer of financial resources as well. As interest rates increased in the early 1980s, and as private bank lending to Latin America declined pro-cyclically in response to the worsening of the current account, net transfers to the region in the years 1982, 1983, and 1984 became negative (for more detailed discussion, see Chapters 3 and 8).

Thus, gross financial flows have not been able to sustain adequate net levels for long periods in the way that developing countries require; this has been linked to the fact that the financial terms on which most of them were contracted (with the exception of an important part of aid flows) were inappropriate for the needs of developing countries, taking the forms most suited to the interests of lenders and investors. As a result, net transfers have often become either low or even negative. Therefore, it can be concluded that, particularly in certain periods, such flows did not fulfil the conditions set by Prebisch and other analysts fundamentally concerned with the Third World's development needs.

The creation and regulation of international liquidity after the Second World War

One of the key features of an international monetary system is the way in which it creates and regulates the supply of reserve assets.

As we saw, a central feature of the Keynes Plan was its ambitious proposal for the creation of an international fiduciary reserve asset, bancor, in very large quantities, and the virtually unlimited obligation of surplus countries to accept payments in bancor; the White Plan (which was the one adopted, given the realities of power) merely envisaged the creation of a pool of *national* currencies and gold from which deficit countries could borrow in limited quantities. In other aspects, the world supply of reserve assets remained unchanged, based on the gold exchange standard.

The gold exchange standard is a system under which reserves consist of gold and foreign exchange, which the reserve centre stands ready to convert into gold on request. When most countries are confident that the reserve currency will not be devalued in relation to gold, they hold a large proportion of their reserves in the form of the reserve currency rather than gold, as the former yields interest and is more convenient for transactions. A strong currency, widely used in international payments, is therefore likely to emerge as a reserve currency, unless the issuing country takes steps to discourage other countries holding its currencies in their reserves. While the reserve centre is concerned to maintain convertibility, the fact that its currency is serving as a reserve currency in theory should not avoid the need to maintain a satisfactory payments position, as failure to do so results in a loss of confidence which is liable to provoke requests for conversion of its currency into gold; in this sense, as Williamson pointed out, 'the economic function of convertibility is, therefore, that of providing a discipline on the policies of the reserve center, analogous to the discipline exerted by the threat of reserve depletion on other countries.'[14]

After the Second World War, gold was the major reserve asset and, it was assumed, would remain so; sterling was still the major reserve currency. The dollar was a reserve currency on a small scale in 1945, but its role expanded rapidly as the US overall balance of payments went into deficit, and as the rest of the world perceived dollars to be as safe as gold, and more convenient in terms of transactions and interest yield. The IMF did play a role in supplementing liquidity, but a very minor one; furthermore, most of the limited liquidity available through the IMF was conditional.

During the 1950s, surplus countries converted part of their dollar earnings into gold and retained the remainder: the key problem then was defined as a 'dollar shortage'. In the early 1960s the term 'dollar problem' shifted from meaning a dollar shortage to a dollar glut; the realization began to emerge that, as a result, the dollar might not remain permanently 'as good as gold'. The essential contradiction of the reserve currency system was clearly articulated in Triffin's influential book, *Gold and the Dollar Crisis*. Triffin's central thesis was that the gold exchange standard contained an inherent dilemma that was ultimately bound to undermine the satisfactory functioning of an international monetary system based on the use of national currencies as international reserves. The 'Triffin Dilemma' was clearly summarized (Triffin, 1978):

If the United States corrected its persistent balance of payments deficits, the growth of world reserves could not be fed adequately by gold production at $35 an ounce, but that if the United States continued to run deficits, its foreign liabilities would inevitably come to exceed by far its ability to convert dollars into gold upon demand and would bring about a 'gold and dollar crisis'.[15]

There was of course a precedent in the problems of an earlier gold exchange standard (based then on sterling) which had collapsed in 1931, prolonging and intensifying the Depression.

Academics, led by Triffin, began in the early 1960s to search for a remedy to this dilemma, which many of them believed could be found by inventing a reserve asset whose supply could be expanded without the need for a US deficit. Probably the most daring of the major proposals was the one advanced by Triffin himself. A central element of the Triffin Plan was the creation of a new 'international reserve currency' to replace the traditional reliance on national currencies as international reserves; control over its supply was to rest with an international agency—a reconstituted IMF—instead of with national authorities. To phase out the use of national currencies as international reserves, existing foreign exchange deposits would be transferred to the reconstituted IMF in exchange for deposit credit there. The reconstituted IMF, however, was to be more than a clearing-house for the settling of accounts. A second central element of the Triffin Plan was the suggestion of mechanisms by which the Fund could create new international reserves, in forms relatively similar to those in which national central banks create reserves for commercial banks. To allay any fear of excesses in deposit creation, special safeguards would be provided to limit such creation.

The academic discussions were later taken up at a more limited (or practical) level by officials in the Group of Ten (the meeting-place of the industrial countries) and the IMF Executive Board. In 1967, there was an agreement to create a new reserve asset called the 'Special Drawing Right', (SDR). Contrary to initial proposals from some industrial countries' Governments to restrict the newly created reserves to an 'inner group of supposedly responsible countries'—the richer ones—it was agreed that such reserves be distributed to all IMF members, proportional to their share in Fund quotas. SDRs relied for their acceptability on the fact that other countries were in turn obliged to accept them, which is the essential basis for the acceptability of money, rather than on support from national currencies or gold.

The agreement was a historic step, as it was the first time that a fiduciary reserve asset had been deliberately created by international agreement. As regards the basic issue of the extent to which the international monetary system contributes to sustain high levels of economic activity at acceptable levels of inflation, the SDR did provide the international community with the ability to create reserves deliberately so as to avoid a reserve shortage, and made reserve creation independent from discoveries of gold or capricious variations in the payments imbalances of reserve centres. Its major limitation, which became crucially important during the 1970s, was *in not providing a constraint on reserve growth through the deficits of reserve centres or the operation of the Euro-currency market*, because SDRs were created in addition to, rather than as a substitute for, gold and foreign exchange (a major difference from the Triffin Plan). Another limitation, which has become apparent only in the early 1980s, is that the decision to issue SDRs is *not* clearly linked to certain technical indicators (for example, level of world reserves or variations of world economic activity), but lies exclusively in the discretionary decisions of the governments which constitute the required majority on the IMF's Executive Board.

The first SDRs were allocated to IMF members at the beginning of January 1970. The supplement to liquidity they provided was rapidly overshadowed by the outflow of dollars from the USA initially reflecting the relaxation of US monetary policy, and which fed on itself as confidence in the dollar waned.

Triffin had been proved right, in that the accumulation of US indebtedness to foreign central banks finally culminated in a gold and dollar crisis; the outcome did not lead—as he had feared—to a drastic reduction in international liquidity and a major recession; the USA did not respond to the confidence crisis, as the UK had in 1931, by trying to maintain a gold exchange standard; by the time world confidence broke, the system had evolved into something much closer to a dollar standard, and the USA was therefore able to suspend convertibility without curtailing international liquidity. What followed was, in fact, an explosive growth in dollar reserves that fuelled world-wide inflation rather than deflation, as the constraints—even though weak—which had been posed by the need to maintain dollar convertibility into gold were eliminated. Thus, the world reserve pool *doubled* from US $79 billion at the end of 1969 to US $159 billion at the endof 1972, 'increasing as much in this short span of three years as in all previous years and centuries since Adam and Eve; world reserves doubled again in the next five years'.[16] The overwhelming source of this increase was foreign exchange holdings, of which traceable dollar and Euro-dollar holdings accounted for more than 80 per cent, having risen nearly twenty times. The SDR and IMF lending contributed a small part of world reserves during the 1970s; the marginal importance of SDRs to total foreign exchange reserves and to their growth is shown by the fact that at the end of 1982 the SDR component was only 2 per cent of total reserves—including gold valued at market prices.[17] This shows that the creation of the SDR, although conceptually important, and offering a potentially significant advance for the international monetary system, has *de facto* made only a marginal contribution to international liquidity.

In fact, it can be argued that, as a consequence of generalized floating of the major currencies since the early 1970s, and the resulting diversification of international reserves—both official and private—so as to reduce risk of currency loss, the international monetary system has *de facto* moved towards a multi-currency reserve system, at the opposite end of the spectrum from an SDR-based system, which it had been hoped would be set in motion with the creation of the SDR.

The trend towards floating of currencies and a multi-currency reserve system, combined with the great expansion in international bank lending during the 1970s, gave a new meaning to international liquidity, which to a certain extent became open-ended. Monetary authorities in industrial countries could enlarge their reserves by buying them in the market; even for countries (such as the developing ones) where this opportunity is not available, central bank reserves could, for certain countries and periods, be readily increased by borrowing from private banks; indeed, holding large reserves often made it easier for countries to borrow still more. Thus, particularly in the 1970s, the supply of international liquidity became—for the industrial and middle-income developing countries —in a gross sense virtually open-ended, subject to creditworthiness. As a result, international control of liquidity became largely a function of the market.

It can therefore be concluded that, even after the creation of the SDR, IMF-created liquidity—either through its own lending or through the issue of SDRs—has played a small role. Furthermore, the elimination of dollar convertibility by the US Government in 1971, accelerated the trend of the main reserve currency centre— the US—to finance huge and persistent deficits by flooding world reserves with its own IOUs. The main mechanism through which these reserves grew and were transmitted during the 1970s, particularly to developing countries, was through the expansion of international commercial lending to sovereign countries. As we will discuss in later chapters, since 1982 debt problems and curtailment in net commercial bank lending—particularly to developing countries—have been making evident the need for a major reconsideration of the role that private banks should and can play, both in the provision of global liquidity requirements and—to look at it from the other side of the coin—in the financing of countries' current account deficits, particularly in the developing world.

The USA, which in the 1970s had large deficits on its capital account, has since 1983 had a large surplus on capital account, which has financed a massive trade deficit; particularly striking is the turnround in banking flows, from net outflows of US $45.1 billion in 1982 to net inflows of US $26.3 billion in 1983.

This point links the discussion of the systemic or global problems of the world monetary system to the specific problems created for developing countries by the nature of the mechanisms and institutions through which liquidity has been mainly created, and transmitted to them, in the last thirty years.

Notes

1. J. M. Keynes, *The General Theory of Employment, Interest and Money*, London, 1936.
2. J. M. Keynes, 'Proposals for an International Currency (or Clearing) Union' (February 1942), reprinted in J. K. Horsefield, ed., *The International Monetary fund, 1945–1965*, vol. 1, *Chronicle*, Washington, DC, 1969.
3. *Ibid.*
4. *Ibid.*
5. Keynes had proposed an amount of 'say 75 per cent' of the average annual sum of each country's exports and imports during the three pre-war years. According to a contemporary estimate by Joan Robinson (1943), this would imply US $26 billion *as a minimum*—if not all countries joined.
6. For this calculation, J. Williamson considers the growth of original member countries' GNP in nominal terms and adds the new membership of the Fund: see 'Keynes and the International Economic Order', paper presented to the conference on 'The Relevance of Keynes's Economics Today' held at King's College, Cambridge, 15–16 July 1983.
7. S. Dell, 'On Being Grandmotherly: The Evolution of IMF Conditionality', *Essays in International Finance* 144, Princeton, 1981.
8. See Foreword by H. Morgenthau (then US Secretary of the Treasury) to the White Plan of 10 July 1943, in Horsefield, ed., *The International Monetary Fund*, vol. 1, p. 86.
9. A brief but interesting historical account can be found in M. Seiber, *International Borrowing by Developing Countries*, Oxford, 1982.
10. Sunkel, 'National Development Policy', op. cit.
11. Raul Prebisch, 'Commercial Policy in the Underdeveloped Countries', *American Economic Review* 49(2), 1959; *Towards a New Trade Policy for Development*, report by the Secretary General of UNCTAD (Raul Prebisch), New York, 1964; and 'La Cooperacion Internacional en el Desarrollo Latinoamericano', in *Problemas Económicos y Sociales de America Latina*, Mundo, 1979.
12. See, for example, Prebisch, 'La Cooperacion Internacional', p. 24.
13. CEPAL preliminary overview of the Latin American economy during 1984, LC/G 1336, January 1985.
14. J. Williamson, *The Failure of World Monetary Reform*, London, 1977.
15. R. Triffin, *Gold and the Dollar Crisis*, New Haven, 1960.
16. R. Triffin *et al.*, 'Experiences and Problems of the International Monetary System', *Economic Notes* 2, Siena, 1982.
17. Commonwealth Secretariat, *Towards a New Bretton-Woods*, London, August 1983.

CHAPTER 5

Financial Flows to Latin America in the 1950s and 1960s

The 1950s and foreign direct investment

As the Second World War came to an end, two developments had an important influence on the future nature of international financial flows: the creation of the Bretton Woods institutions, and the great weight of the USA in the world economy.

As discussed in Chapter 4, the 1944 Conference of Bretton Woods had agreed on the need for international consultation and co-operation on monetary matters. The two Bretton Woods institutions—the IMF and the World Bank—were created as part of an attempt to avoid the instability of exchange rates, the financial chaos that had accompanied the World Depression of the 1930s, and the protective controls and competitive devaluations of the inter-war period. Bretton Woods—and the institutions it created—represented the first coherent attempt at imposing order and stability on the world monetary system and preserving its unity as a single system. The financial order emerging from Bretton Woods, initially reflected the 1930s disenchantment with *laissez-faire* in financial transactions which had then had such negative effects; it was to a certain extent influenced by Fabian/New Deal notions.

It is important to note here that Latin American nations were the main group of developing countries to participate at the Bretton Woods discussions and to join the Bretton Woods institutions soon after they were established. Thus, nineteen Latin American countries (Bolivia, Brazil, Chile, Colombia, Costa Rica, Cuba, Dominican Republic, Ecuador, El Salvador, Guatemala, Honduras, Mexico, Nicaragua, Panama, Paraguay, Peru, Uruguay, Venezuela) joined the IMF before the end of 1946, while only eight developing countries from the rest of the world joined at the time—China, Egypt, Ethiopia, India, Iran, Iraq, the Philippines, and Yugoslavia.[1] As is well known, at the time of the setting up of the Bretton Woods institutions, many of the countries today called developing were still colonies.

The attempt at control of the world monetary system by official international institutions at the time was, however, not accompanied in practice by large financial flows from them, particularly to the developing countries. As Lamfalussy has pointed out, the main feature of international capital movements during the years which followed the Second World War was the large outflow of funds from the USA.[2] During the late 1940s and the 1950s, the USA was clearly richer and stronger than ever before, and was the only country able to offer both economic aid and military protection. Even though it controlled the Bretton Woods institutions, the United States preferred bilateral channels for its financial flows. More importantly, the original Fabian Social Democratic notions which were evident at Bretton Woods were increasingly pushed into the background once the war was over.

Since the Second World War, Latin American representatives had been appealing for a regional aid programme of substantial proportions, on similar lines to the Marshall Plan. Probably the most coherent and concrete of these Latin American proposals was elaborated at the 1954 Inter-American Economic and Social Meeting at Quintadinha, inspired by Prebisch and the thinking of CEPAL. The main proposals included the creation of an Inter-American Bank, a level of annual foreign assistance and aid to Latin America of US $1 billion, the development of national planning, and commodity price stabilization. The proposals, as well as later similar ones, were consistently rejected by representatives both of the Truman and of the Eisenhower Administrations. The main reason (explicitly given in US official documents) was that Latin America played at the time a very secondary role in the Cold War. US officials recommended instead that Latin America concentrate on improving the climate for private foreign investment, basically through control of inflation, adhering *strictly* to what A. Schlesinger has called the 'theory of development as an act of immaculate private conception'.[3] These recommendations ring a very familiar bell in the early 1980s, when once again the US Administration and orthodox circles in general lay great emphasis on the need for Latin American countries to improve the climate for foreign investment. For example, in a *Financial Times* editorial,[4] it is argued that developing countries should scrap import-substituting protectionist policies . . . as a non-protectionist LDC which can offer multinationals a low-wage base from which to attack world markets has a good chance of attracting foreign equity capital, . . . [they should] welcome wholly foreign-owned subsidiaries and giving their managements a free hand by eliminating 'bureaucratic' controls and overcoming their fixation with controlling the profits stream of foreign investors and . . . follow 'credible' macroeconomic policies, as multinationals will not invest if they fear a sudden clamp down on profit repatriation because of a foreign exchange constraint.

Again in 1985, as in the 1950s, developing countries' governments are being told that they must yield, in body and soul, to the dictates of international financial institutions and to the desires of foreign investors, so as to obtain the 'privilege' of attracting foreign equity.

Both bilateral and multilateral official institutions played a negligible role during the 1950s. As can be seen in Table 5.1, financial flows to Latin America were mainly in the form of private direct investment by multinational corporations. The import substitution policies of the Latin American countries provided them with profitable business. Investment was then protected by high tariff barriers, and credit was obtainable on favourable terms. Multinational corporations jumped the high tariff barriers in these countries by setting up or buying enterprises in the Latin American countries. This contributed strongly to the beginning of

Table 5.1. US capital movements 1946–61, total and to Latin America (US $ billion)

	1946–8^a		1949–55^a		1956–61^a	
	Total	Latin America	Total	Latin America	Total	Latin America
US capital (net)	−3.52	−0.38	−1.30	−0.33	−4.12	−0.99
Private	−0.77	−0.32	−1.04	−0.24	−3.30	−0.69
Government	−2.75	−0.06	−0.26	−0.09	−0.82	−0.30

Source: US Department of Commerce, *Balance of Payments Supplement*, Washington, DC, 1961.
Note:
a. Annual averages.

a process of transnationalization of production, which subsequently extended to patterns of consumption, life-styles, and culture.[5]

A new period of international economic integration—as had existed before the 1930s depression—was emerging, this time with a transnational character; it had begun with the post-war recovery of international trade and the related transfer of consumption patterns, continued with the expansion of transnational private investment and patterns of technology and production, and was to culminate in the creation of a transnational financial market of a private character (see Chapter 6). Increasingly, the development of the private transnational financial system grew far faster than the internationalization of public regulatory and supervisory rules designed to control it; similarly, privately transferred liquidity to LDCs would grow far faster, from the 1970s onwards, than flows intermediated by public international institutions.

Returning to the post-war period, Table 5.1 shows that during the years 1946 to 1961, US net private capital flows to Latin America were much higher than official flows; this was even more marked in the first ten years after the war, as during the second half of the 1950s US official flows to Latin America began to increase.

In 1950, approximately half of US foreign direct investment was in the so-called developing countries, and over 40 per cent was concentrated in Latin America. The share going to developing countries systematically declined between 1950 and 1979, mainly as a result of the fall in the share of investment in Latin America (see Table 5.2). This decline was more rapid during the late 1950s and the 1960s.

The changing shares in the composition of North American investment occurred in the context of rapid growth of total US direct investment abroad during the period 1950–79 (at an annual nominal rate of 10.1 per cent). Although American foreign investment was growing very rapidly, the share going to developing countries (and to Latin America in particular) declined substantially as US multinational corporations found more profitable and/or more 'secure' investment opportunities in other industrial countries, particularly in Europe. US direct investment in developing countries grew relatively more slowly during the 1960s than in other decades. This was due to developments both in the industrialized and in the third world countries. In developing

Table 5.2. US direct investment position abroad
(Percentage composition by area)

	1950	1957	1966	1979[a]
All areas	100.0	100.0	100.0	100.0
Developed countries	48.0	55.1	68.1	71.6
Developing countries	48.0	40.5	26.8	24.8
Latin America	(40.6)	(31.4)	(18.9)	(19.1)
Others	4.0	3.4	5.1	4.6

Source: Data taken from US Department of Commerce, *Survey of Current Business*, Washington, DC, February 1981.
Notes:
a. Choice of years if based on those for which the information reflects a bench-mark survey, whereas intermediate years are based only on sample information. For explanation, see O. G. Whichard, 'Trends in the US Direct Investment Position Abroad, 1950–79', in *Survey of Current Business* (see above).

countries, the issue of foreign control became increasingly sensitive; this was reflected in expropriations and prohibitions of entry into sectors such as natural resources and telecommunications. On the other hand, the US Government imposed both voluntary and mandatory controls on outflows of capital to protect the balance of payments. Such controls particularly affected inter-company outflows.

An important trend which emerged in the composition of US investment during the period 1950–79 was that reinvestment of earnings grew while equity and inter-company flows declined; in fact, during five of the eight years from 1972 to 1979, absolute declines in inter-company flows were registered.[6] It is, of course, only the inter-company outflows which imply a transfer of financial resources to other countries. The relative decline in the proportion of total US investment which went to Latin America, the diminishing importance of inter-company flows, as well as the rising level of profit remittances by US companies, implies that already in the 1960s the total net flow of direct private capital from the US into Latin America was negative. Thus, between 1961 and 1968, net direct investment minus profit remittances of US companies in Latin America amounted to −US $5.7 billion.[7]

In the late 1940s and the 1950s, private flows predominantly took the form of direct investment. The international financial and money markets had not yet recovered from the shocks they had suffered during the Great Depression. Private credit flows were small, and mainly the result of credit provided by suppliers for the purchase of equipment. Thus, in Latin America, in 1960, of total debt to private creditors, 48 per cent was owed to suppliers.[8]

The 1960s and official aid

Towards the mid-1950s, the American attitude towards official aid began to change rapidly. As Christopher Prout pointed out, '[the increase in aid] *motivation was unashamedly political*'.[9] Americans believed that 'contributing to the economic and social development of the uncommitted nations would lead to the growth of societies sympathetic to their way of life'. The turning point for US aid to Latin America was the Cuban Revolution in 1959, and the subsequent launching of a massive aid programme under the Alliance for Progress. However, the mid-1950s had already seen the beginning of a debate, carried out within the USA amongst 'internationalists' and 'isolationists', about expanded economic assistance, which acquired importance during the 1957 hearings of the US Senate on the subject. On this occasion, the Committee on Economic Development (a research-lobby group mainly composed of major multinational corporation executives and representatives of the press, created in the early 1950s) strongly supported increased foreign aid.

There is agreement amongst different writers that the 1959 Cuban Revolution marked a qualitatively significant turning-point in US attitudes towards Latin America, which had a predominant influence on the magnitude and nature of aid, which was part of the Alliance for Progress. Washington became increasingly anxious that, through Cuba's example and international efforts, revolution might rapidly spread through Latin America. It became fashionable to view the whole of Latin America as facing only two alternatives: reform or revolution.[10] The USA needed swiftly to bring all its influence to bear to ensure that the first alternative prevailed. John Kennedy many times repeated that 'the promotion of democracy and reform were the ultimate answers to Castro and the communists'. The new administration believed that economic development and social reform, spurred by North American aid, could blunt the appeal of radicalism.

More broadly, the Alliance for Progress programme, and in particular its initial rhetoric, was highly influenced by a very important segment of Latin American thinking. The Quintadinha proposals mentioned earlier provided the first blueprint for the Alliance. Of particular influence during the early stages of the Alliance was the memorandum written by Prebisch, Mayobre, Felipe Herrera, and other eminent Latin American economists and delivered to President Kennedy just before he launched his new programme. It called on the USA to co-operate with those Latin American countries willing to make structural social and economic changes (with particular emphasis on land tenure, education, and tax reform); to capture the support of the masses, by convincing them 'with clear and palpable evidence that the program is not motivated by a desire to create lucrative fields of investment for foreign private capital', and to launch an external programme of long-term supplementary capital assistance and commodity price stabilization.

The initial rhetoric of the Alliance was thus very enlightened. As can be seen from President Kennedy's initial speech, and from the Charter of Punta del Este itself, there were three officially stated goals to the programme: economic growth, structural change, and political democratization. Furthermore, it was said that structural change and political democratization would be a condition for USA economic aid.

Even though these progressive aims were the officially stated goals of the Alliance, the real aims pursued were somewhat different. As we saw, the Alliance (and the large increase in American aid which it implied) were to a great extent a reaction to the Cuban Revolution; this is made completely explicit in the writings both of 'liberal' historians and of politicians. For example, Levinson and Onis recognize that 'the predominant objective of US policy in the Alliance for Progress was to prevent other Latin American countries from following the example of Cuba'.[11] 'Liberal' historians stress initial (though unusual and temporary) absence of corporate influence in the Alliance for Progress programme. They correctly point out that the programme, drafted by international civil servants, academic specialists, and politicians, made hardly any reference to US private investment.

This attitude was by no means an oversight, but a deliberate response from the Kennedy Administration to the warning given by Latin American economists not to appear as furthering interests of US foreign investors through the Alliance.

It should be pointed out, however, that big business was not as absent in the birth of the Alliance as the 'liberals' claim. Dillon, who headed the US mission to Punta del Este, was an international banker. One of the strongest defenders of the Alliance in the US Congress was the international banker David Rockefeller who, during that whole decade, headed the lobby of US business interests in Latin America. Furthermore, and perhaps more importantly, there had been a significant shift since the late 1950s; North American big business, and in particular the multinationals, were clearly shifting to favour and support increase in US foreign aid.

After Kennedy's death, US policy towards Latin America became both more conservative and more fragmented. Thomas Mann, named by Johnson as both co-ordinator of the Alliance and Assistant Secretary for Inter-American Affairs, set forth the new line early in 1964. As Levinson and Onis say: 'What became known as the Mann doctrine consisted of four main objectives: (1) to foster economic growth and be neutral on social reform; (2) to protect US private investments in the hemisphere; (3) to show no preference, through aid or otherwise, for representative democratic institutions; and (4) to oppose Communism.' Thus, both structural reforms and democracy stopped being official aims of the Alliance, while the protection of US private investments in the hemisphere became an explicit goal of the Alliance.

By the end of 1966, US policy in Latin America was clearly in its more pragmatic phase, favourable both to the military and 'modernizing' governments and to the democratic and 'reformist' governments. As the 1960s finish, the emphasis is increasingly shifting towards the 'modernizers'.

As can be seen in Table 5.3, the total level of gross US economic assistance to Latin America during the 1960s was rather impressive, exceeding US \$10 billion for the period 1961–9. However, net disbursements were substantially smaller. Over half of gross economic assistance was devoted to repayments, amortization of previous loans, and interests. American official credits and aid were supposed to finance government investment programmes.

Table 5.3. Economic assistance and private capital flows between the USA and Latin America in the 1960s (US $ million)

Total gross economic assistance to Latin America 1961–9^a	Total net US direct disbursements to Latin America 1961–6^b	Total net flow of private capital from USA into Latin America 1961–8^c
10,286	4,819	−5,738

Source: S. Griffith-Jones, 'The Alliance for Progress: An Attempt at Interpretation', *Development and Change* 10(3), July 1979.
Notes:
a. Includes all AID funds, Food for Freedom, long-term export–import bank loans, and other US economic programmes. (Excludes assistance from international agencies where USA is an important contributor.) Refers to obligations and loan authorizations.
b. Includes same items as (*a*), but refers to net disbursements, (*a*) less repayments and interests.
c. Net direct investment less profit remittances to USA.

However, if the total financial flows between the USA and Latin America are considered, it becomes evident that the net transfer of US private investment funds from Latin America to the USA (which includes net direct investment minus profit remittances) *exceeded* the net inflow of US official funds. This trend is perhaps the main factor which explains the support of US multinationals for the Alliance for Progress, even though naturally it cannot be deduced mechanically that official aid financed outflow of foreign private capital.

As was the case for foreign direct investment, the initiative for the flow of official assistance came from the USA. As can be seen in Table 5.4, during the first half of the 1960s, nearly all bilateral official flows to Latin America came from the USA. US bilateral aid was then the largest source of net external finance for Latin America. Gradually other industrial countries came into the scene, partly as a result of the American desire to persuade its affluent allies to share more equitably the financial burden of allegedly common foreign policy objectives. American attempts to persuade its allies were mainly carried out through OECD, the Organisation for Economic Cooperation and Development; the

Table 5.4. Structure and level of net inflow of external resources to Latin America[a] 1961–8

% Structure	Annual averages				1976	1977	1978
	1961–5	1966–70	1971–5				
I Net Public inflow	60.2	40.1	25.2		19.6	12.0	7.3
A. Multilateral	19.5	15.7	13.4		14.4	7.4	3.1
1. Development	16.6	17.1	11.6		6.6	8.4	7.2
2. Compensatory	2.9	−1.4	1.8		7.8	−1.0	−4.1
B. Bilateral	40.7	24.4	11.8		5.2	4.6	4.2
1. USA	36.9	23.6	6.8		2.6	1.7	0.8
2. Other countries[b]	3.8	0.8	5.0		2.6	2.9	3.4
II Net private inflow[c]	39.8	59.9	74.8		80.4	88.0	92.7
A. Banks[d]	2.1	9.3	43.8		61.0	48.3	56.6
B. Suppliers	7.7	13.8	2.3		3.7	5.8	9.8
C. Bonds	5.0	2.5	2.5		3.3	14.8	10.3
D. Direct investment	25.2	33.3	26.2		12.4	20.1	16.0
III Total %	100.0	100.0	100.0		100.0	100.0	100.0
Total actual level (US $ million)	1,575.8	2,641.3	7,561.9		15,301.5	15,637.0	21,807.2

Source: Calculations based on data in Inter-American Development Bank, *Economic and Social Progress in Latin America 1979 Report*, Washington, DC, 1979.
Notes:
a. Includes the member countries of the Inter-American Development Bank and the sub-regional agencies.
b. Includes the socialist countries and the OECD members except the USA.
c. Includes credits for nationalization.
d. Includes financial institutions other than banks.

establishment of the OECD's Development Assistance Committee in 1961 was tangible evidence of such American pressure. When America's interest in its official bilateral aid programme declined in the mid-1960s, other industrial countries (particularly the smaller ones) were increasing their aid programmes. As is show in Table 5.4, by the mid-1970s US net official flows to Latin America were smaller than those from other industrialized countries, which contrasts sharply with the picture in the early 1960s.

Similarly, multilateral development official flows to Latin America began largely at the initiative of the US Government. It had a leading role in the creation of, and establishment of initial finance for, both the World Bank in 1945 and the Inter-American Development Bank in 1959. These, too, acquired a dynamic of their own. Thus, although during the 1970s the contribution of net multilateral development official flows declined relatively as a source of finance, their decline was much less than that of US net bilateral public flows.

To summarize, official aid in the 1960s was predominantly an American initiative; it responded largely to foreign policy interests of the USA, even though the financial needs of Latin American countries played a part in the determination of the magnitude and composition of aid. Aid, albeit unintentionally, compensated for the net outflow of foreign direct investment. The US initiative was later followed—and surpassed—by other industrial countries. Like foreign direct investment, aid became a 'transnational' initiative.

At another level, it seems that the 'real' Alliance was not based—as liberal historians still claim—mainly on the 'progressive north and south'; nor was its nature accurately expressed in the rhetoric of Punta del Este. The 'real' Alliance was expressed much more clearly by the language of Johnson and his Administration; it was basically an alliance between the interests of international business and the more dynamic private and public entrepreneurs in Latin America.[12]

The direct interests of individual US multinationals were initially subordinated to 'hemispheric security' (anti-Communist) considerations. However, as the 'subversive threat' receded, these direct interests came more clearly to the front.

From the point of view of Latin American private and state entrepreneurs, the Alliance for Progress helped support the last stage of their import substitution model. Undoubtedly, Alliance aid helped provide resources for building infrastructure, and social and productive investment necessary for the sustainment of this model.

As we shall discuss in the next chapter, despite its deficiencies, official aid—such as was granted by the Alliance during the 1960s—implied the consideration of important social criteria and avoided open abuses (such as massive use of flows for capital flight), which made its impact on the welfare of the majority of the people in the aid-recipient countries far more positive than that of private flows in the 1970s.

Notes

1. IMF, *International Financial Statistics, Supplement on Fund Accounts*, Supplement Series 3, Washington, DC, 1982.
2. A. Lamfalussy, 'Changing Attitudes Towards Capital Movements', paper presented at the conference on 'Changing Perceptions of Economic Policy', Oxford, 27–9 March 1981.
3. A. Schlesinger, 'The Alliance for Progress: A Perspective', in R. G. Hillman and H. J. Rosenbaum, eds., *Latin America: The Search for a New International Role*, Chichester, 1975.
4. 'Investment in the Third World', *Financial Times*, 21 March 1985.
5. See Ch. 3 above, and O. Sunkel and E. Fuenzalida, 'Transnationalism and its National Consequences', in J. Villamil, ed., *Transnational Capitalism and National Development*, Brighton, 1979 (Spanish version, Mexico City, 1982).
6. US Department of Commerce, *Survey of Current Business*, Washington, DC, February 1981.
7. J. Levinson and J. Onis, *The Alliance That Lost Its Way: A Critical Report on the Alliance for Progress*, Chicago, 1970, p. 120.
8. Inter-American Development Bank, *Economic and Social Progress in Latin America*, Washington, DC, 1979, Table 59.
9. C. Prout, 'Finance for Developing Countries: An Essay', in S. Strange, ed., *International Monetary Relations*, vol. 2 of *International Economic Relations of the Western World*, ed. A. Schonfield, Oxford, 1976, p. 361.
10. See, for example, Schlesinger, 'The Alliance for Progress'.
11. Levinson and Onis, *The Alliance That Lost Its Way*.
12. Osvaldo Sunkel, 'Esperando a Godot: America Latina ante la Nueva Administracion Republicana de los Estados Unidos', *Estudios Internacionales* 3(1), Santiago de Chile.

CHAPTER 6

The Privatization of the International Financial System in the 1970s and its Implications

A broad historical perspective

In our opinion, there is a close relation between the degree of integration or disintegration of the international economy—and in particular of the international financial markets—and the degree of protectionism or openness of the national economies, their resource allocation criteria, their options between consumption and investment, the form taken by their power structures, and the degree of state intervention, all of which is reflected in conceptual and economic policy formulations.

During the period of outward-looking development, which extended from the nineteenth century up to 1930, there was a close economic, commercial, and financial integration at the international level, which resulted in the predominance of the pound sterling—a currency which enjoyed strong economic as well as military backing—and found expression in wide and increasing international flows of trade, credit, investment, and even migration. This world-wide establishment of the British Empire and its zones of influence, such as Latin America, was acommpanied by national situations of little protection and very open economies, both at the centre and at the periphery. This led to a process of allocating resources according to comparative advantages. As the comparative advantages acquired by the centre were concentrated mainly in manufacturing industry, its export trade became specialized in manufactures, and as the countries of the periphery had not gained similar advantages, they specialized in sectors characterized by intensive use of natural resources and labour.

To this structural situation corresponded a specific organization of political power: a dominant coalition was formed by the exporter sectors (manufacturers at the centre, raw materials producers at the periphery), the importer sectors (raw materials in the centre, manufactured goods at the periphery), the big businessmen, and, above all, the financial sectors. The interest of the latter in maximizing international trade and finance resulted in relatively little state intervention in the economy, except for the purposes of creating the infrastructure services required by the outward-looking growth model, or imposing the rules of the game. *Laissez-faire* policies predominated, as well as their rationalization in ideological and theoretical terms—that is, in terms of the classic liberal theory of market allocation of resources both at the national and at the international level (static theory of comparative advantages).

This stage of capitalist development ended in the Great Depression of 1930, followed by a long interregnum preceding the US hegemony that arose after the Second World War. During this period some profound readjustments took place: international markets disintegrated; the international private financial market disappeared, as did direct private investment; and trade flows were reduced. The generalized crisis in trade, finance, and international private investment was manifested in all countries in serious imbalances on their international transactions, and in a severe depression of economic activity. Most countries withdrew from the international system, and isolated their economies by applying protectionist measures in the field of trade and exchange controls in the field of finance.

It is important to stress that this protectionism occurred simultaneously in the centre and in the periphery. Import substitution was not a perverse invention of the peripheral countries, or of Prebisch and ECLA, as some economists of little historical culture seem to believe: it was also, and at the same time, the recourse to which the central countries turned in order to meet the crisis. Each country protected and encouraged what it had formerly imported: the central countries essentially protected their agriculture, and thence arose a whole institutional apparatus of support and promotion of agriculture which is still—fifty years later—a very serious obstacle to international trade and the agricultural production of the Third World.

In Latin American and Caribbean countries, the 1930 crisis led to generalized protection of manufacturing, and marked the beginning of a phase of deliberate development of import-substituting industry. A gap was thus created between the internal and the international price systems, reflected in a change in the relative prices of agricultural commodities and industrial goods. Consequently, an adjustment took place in the allocation of resources: at the periphery, towards the development of manufacturing and at the centre, towards agricultural development. This process did not happen automatically, but through decisive state action and a rearticulation, in both types of countries, of the hegemonic coalition of power within the ruling classes. The coalition dominated by exporter, importer, business, and financial interests, was ousted—not without radical political conflicts—by a coalition based mainly on entrepreneurial sectors, middle-class groups, and the organized working classes, a change that was reflected in the importance attached to production, employment, and income distribution in overcoming the crisis.

These were the decades from the 1930s to the 1960s, which were characterized in many Latin American countries by governments that subscribed to active state intervention in support of industrial development; investment in infrastructure; some structural reforms; income redistribution through in increase in social expenditure; and public policies favouring the middle-income and low-income groups.[1] In the international field, regional integration and co-operation were actively fostered, as were public technical and economic co-operation between developed and underdeveloped countries.

With the appropriate reservations, the post-war picture of the industrialized countries—the USA, the European countries, and Japan—is not so very different. There, too, the state assumed a leading role in the reactivation and reconstruction of the economy; the correction of unfair income distribution by application of the concept of a welfare state; and the adoption of systematic full-employment policies. In Europe, moreover, very marked emphasis was placed on regional integration and co-operation.

The institutional modernization of the state and the practice of planning figured in both developed and developing areas as guiding instruments that modified and complemented the market. The economic theories in vogue revolved around economic growth in the centre and development policies in Latin America, where the subject of planning acquired outstanding importance. Theoretical discussion was focused on criticism of traditional neoclassical and Keynesian (static) economic theory, in relation to the need for a growth theory (dynamic and post-Keynesian), structural change, and development.

While this was occurring on the internal stage, the international economic system was also trying to recover from the 1930s *débâcle*. During the next decade, international trade revived, but private investment, both direct and financial, had completely disappeared. Instead, some public institutions were set up, such as Eximbank in the USA, to facilitate export expansion. As described in Chapter 4, an international financial system of a public character was created under the Bretton Woods agreements, including, in particular, the World Bank and the IMF. To these organizations were later added other public international institutions, such as the regional development banks, the public bilateral and multilateral financial aid institutions, and the state agencies responsible for guaranteeing export credits.

As described in Chapter 5, during the 1950s and 1960s direct international private investment reappeared, now embodied in the transnational corporations, which at first were solely North American, and later European and Japanese as well. This was the start of a process of transnationalization of the structure of production, which extended later to patterns of consumption, life-styles, and culture. The end of the 1960s saw the first steps in the re-creation of an international private financial market, whose expansion during the following decade attained extraordinary dimensions. A new period of international economic integration—this time of a transnational character—now dawned, beginning with the recovery of trade and the transfer of patterns of consumption and life-styles, continuing with the expansion of transnational private investment and patterns of technology and production, and culminating, especially after 1973, in the creation of a transnational financial market of a private character which had great freedom of manœuvre, as it grew to an important extent in the gaps between national regulatory and supervisory authorities.

The main features in external financial flows to Latin America in the 1970s

It is of interest here to underline central characteristics of external financial flows to developing countries during the 1970s, with particular reference to Latin America.

1. As was seen in Table 5.4, since the late 1960s the proportion of external finance coming to Latin America from private sources increased dramatically from 39.8 per cent in 1961–5 to 92.7 per cent in 1978; this implied the growth of private net flows from an annual average of US $627 million in the period 1961–5 to US $20,205 million in 1978. (Even though part of this increase reflects US inflation, the growth in real terms of net private flows is dramatic.) The relative and absolute increase of private flows to Asia and Africa was also very great, though not as spectacular as the growth in respect to Latin America.

2. The second change is related to the composition of such private flows. As can be seen in Table 5.4, during the 1960s private funds were predominantly direct investments (although, as discussed above, the *net* flow of foreign investment was already negative, owing to the outflow of profits). Since the 1970s, multinational banks have provided the main source of flows, and these have surpassed both direct investment and public funds.

Net private credits from multinational banks to Latin America have risen from an annual average of US $246 million in 1966–70 to US $12,348 in 1978—that is, an increase of more than fifty times in a period of approximately ten years. This feature follows the general trend for all developing countries, but it is much more marked in Latin America, where a very high proportion of total credits have been concentrated. According to data from the Bank for International Settlements (1981), in December 1980, of accumulated net total lending by multinational banks to non-OPEC developing countries, over 80 per cent went to Latin America. This rapidly growing proportion of net external finance arising from international banks has naturally led to the 'privatization' of the debt structure of developing countries.

3. A third feature was the oligopolization of the international capital market, implicit in the 1970s but which became particularly evident after 1982. The copious inflow of credit into many countries was organized in the 1970s by some thirty big transnational banks, which obtained a considerable proportion of the financing from several hundreds of small- and medium-sized banks through the system of syndicated loans, acting in a competitive capital market. Since 1982, for the purpose mainly of managing the debt crisis and sustaining lending, but also to obtain monopoly rents from the renegotiation of debts, the seven or eight largest

transnational banks have organized themselves into *ad hoc* steering committees; there has been since that date substantial organized co-ordination among these large banks, national authorities, and multilateral financial institutions (particularly the IMF), which to a certain extent have 'created a market', of often 'involuntary' lending. Since 1982, not only has the competitive element been dramatically reduced from the international private capital market for practically all Latin American countries, but also the very existence of a normal market has been put in doubt by some analysts, as the system is to such a large extent administered by major actors (for more details, see Chapter 8).

4. A fourth important trend is that, as can be seen in Table 5.4, during the 1970s—and particularly since 1973—there was a very dramatic increase in the nominal and real level of total net financial flows to Latin America. Although partly boosting foreign exchange reserves, these loans were used mainly to cover the rapidly growing deficits in balance of payments current account. The large deficits resulting from the exhaustion of the import substitution model were greatly increased by the jump in the international price of oil and of other imported goods, coupled with reduced demand for their exports due to the recession in the industrialized countries. The current account deficits of Latin American countries (and particularly the oil-importing ones) increased substantially in the 1973–81 period (see Table 6.1); thus the current account balance of Latin America grew almost fourfold in two years, from US $3.5 billion in 1973 to US $14 billion in 1975; it increased dramatically again between 1978 and 1980.

5. A fifth new feature of financial flows after 1973 was that members of OPEC in some years replaced the industrial countries as net suppliers of capital, as can be seen in Table 6.2. Thus the shortfall of national savings over domestic investment in the oil-importing world was met by the savings surplus of the oil exporters. The main conduit for 'recycling' this large volume of funds from surplus to deficit countries was, however, the private multinational banking system of the industrial countries.

6. A sixth feature was the very limited response during the 1970s of public international institutions—and particularly of the IMF—to the magnitude of the balance of payments problems of oil-importing LDCs. It has perhaps not been sufficiently stressed

Table 6.1. Current account balance of Latin America, 1973–84 (US $ billion)

1973	1974	1975	1976	1977	1978
−3.2	−7.4	−14.0	−11.0	−11.8	−18.3

1979	1980	1981	1982	1983	1984
−19.5	−28.1	−40.5	−40.4	−9.3	−3.1

Sources: For 1973–83, CEPAL, *Estudio Economico de America Latina y el Caribe*, 1983; for 1984, preliminary figures in ECLAC, *Preliminary Overview of the Latin American Economy*, Santiago de Chile, January 1985.

in the literature that in the period 1973–82, the IMF, through all its facilities, financed a mere 3.1 per cent of the current account deficits of non-oil developing countries.[2] The IMF is often criticized for its actions in relation to particular countries; perhaps its main defects, however, lie in its omissions as regards the needs of the global economy!

7. Furthermore, during the 1970s, there was an almost total lack of public control and supervision with respect to the process of expansion of private international lending. The 'sins of omission' of the industrial governments, and of institutions like the IMF, also imply that the responsibility for the debt crisis should be shared by the transnational banks, the governments of the industrial countries where these banks have headquarters, and the governments of the over-indebted countries.

The governments, particularly of the OPEC countries and of the third world in general, wasted a unique opportunity to use their leverage more to attempt to convert the obsolete Bretton Woods institutions into an international public system genuinely representative of the interests of the community of nations, accountable to their governments, and directed towards promoting the development of the third world and preserving the dynamism and stability of the international economy.

Just as Monsieur Jourdain spoke prose unawares, throughout the 1970s we have lived through the equivalent of a Marshall Plan,

Table 6.2. The pattern of global capital flows^a (US \$ billion)

	$1967–73^a$	$1974–7^b$	1978	1979	1980
Group of Ten countries and Switzerland	-8.25	-0.75	-19.5	23.5	51.5
Smaller developed countries	1.5	17.75	10.5	12	22
Non-oil developing countries	6	21	22.5	36	51
Oil-exporting countries	-1.25	-38	-4.5	-68	-116

Source: Lamfalussy, 'Changing Attitudes Towards Capital Movements', based on IMF and OECD data.
Notes:
a. Total capital flows including monetary movements (i.e. current account positions with the sign reversed); minus signs indicate capital export.
b. Annual averages.

without referring to it or even noticing it. The recommendations of the Brandt Commission were in fact applied, but *avant la lettre*, in accordance with market criteria, and by the transnational banks, instead of by a public international mechanism, responsible and under the control of the national states. The result was, on the one hand, a fundamental Keynesian contribution by the multinational banks to the maintenance of some degree of expansion of the international economy during the 1970s, which enabled the latter partly to overcome its trend towards stagnation from the end of the 1960s (see Chapter 7), and, on the other hand, a colossal waste of productive resources during that period, since these financial flows were allocated, in part at least, to financing pharaonic and over-sized investment projects which have been left incomplete or are only partially in use, to a great increase in luxury consumption, to the production and purchase of armaments, and even to flight of capital and corruption.

This problematic situation contrasts with that of the public international financial system and, in general, with the whole of the international system of bilateral and multilateral co-operation and aid for development which prevailed in the 1950s and 1960s. That mechanism, despite all its limitations and deficiencies, implied certain social criteria as regards anti-cyclical stabilization and resource allocation policies, which were superseded in the 1970s by pure private and market criteria, and, in the last analysis, in many cases by sheer lack of judgement. Under the first system referred to, the allocation of international public financial resources was subject to state mediation both in the donor and the recipient countries. Public resource allocation criteria were established which reflected long-term sociopolitical options, such as promoting industrial development, providing basic social capital, introducing structural reforms and modernizing agriculture, saving foreign exchange, and creating employment. These were criteria which the parliaments of the developed countries imposed upon their own states and their foreign aid and financing institutions, and on the basis of which the state of the underdeveloped country negotiated, in so far as this state reflected long-term national interests.

On the contrary, market criteria correspond to the maximization of profits in the minimum possible length of time, and reflect to an excessive extent the consumer preferences of the high-income groups, and the market strategies of the most powerful and dynamic national and transnational private groups. Here there is a difference of fundamental importance: governments and entrepreneurs have had great freedom to obtain and allocate vast quantities of external resources, but this increased freedom has not necessarily been to the advantage of the countries receiving that plentiful inflow of private capital. Apart from the problems of higher and particularly variable financial cost which such an inflow represents, which we will discuss in the following sections, the problem lies first in the fact that, when the governments concerned are not firmly committed to a development policy, the readily available supply of short-term external private financing may take the place of long-term external and internal savings, and is diverted to consumption, instead of helping to broaden and diversify productive capacity; and secondly, in the fact that the market by itself is often not the most appropriate instrument for channelling resources towards the development of a diversified production system, accompanied by social justice, and sustainable over the long term.

In cases where the state continued to control the allocation of resources for development, in face of the abundance of external resources it often lost all sense of prudence and moderation and sank into a kind of financial fools' paradise, forgetting that real institutional and human capacity for rational utilization of financial resources is limited, and that disproportionate short-term external borrowing is never an appropriate base for development strategy. In the petroleum-exporting countries, another great mirage took the form of confusing structural adjustments in petroleum prices with a sustained long-term trend, and of basing on the former the wildest investment projects and a reckless boosting of consumption. It would seem that all these issues, fully discussed in the literature of development, were likewise forgotten in the great financial conjuring act of the 1970s.

Furthermore, transnational financial integration, the restoration of easy and ample access to the international private financial system, and the possibility of large-scale borrowing exerted strong pressure in favour of adopting policies of openness and liberalization in trade and finance. When the political conflict between different coalitions is defined in these terms, the result is—as has occurred in different degrees in most Latin American countries—over-expansion of imports of consumer goods, and of the commercial and financial services sectors, and a reallocation of resources to the sectors with natural comparative advantages—including, in some countries, activities with advantages acquired during the import substitution process. All this was accompanied by an attempt to consolidate the new hegemonic coalition: supported by international private financing, and under the leadership of the financial sector, exporters and importers entered upon the scene with renewed vigour, seeking to take the place of the coalition formed by the industrial sectors, middle-income groups, and working classes. There was a definite effort to reduce state intervention in order to leave the market—that is, the main economic groups—to operate as freely as posssible, an updating of *laissez-faire* policies and the whole market ideology of free exchange, static comparative advantage, private enterprise, and individualism. All this, of course, took place with the energetic backing of the new transnational centres of financial power.

A particularly negative development linked to the abundance of foreign lending and unrestricted convertibility in Latin American countries was greatly increased capital flight; particularly for some Latin American countries, such capital flight became in the early 1980s an important part of the increase in their foreign debt. As public debt was turned into private assets for a minority of 'transnationalised citizens', these benefited from tax evasion and high interest rates—which the transnational banks offered them— while their far poorer and less mobile fellow nationals had to bear the burden of adjustment which would make servicing of the same external debt possible. As Diaz-Alejandro has pointed out,[3] this situation reduces the political legitimacy of efforts to service the external debt, and has even generated a crisis of legitimacy for the role of the private sector in Latin American development.

In a commentary written on the eve of the crisis, the following questions were propounded. How long will the pendulum stay at the extreme of transnational financial integration on which the strategy of external openness is so decidedly based? How far can the already taut cord of private external borrowing be stretched, especially in view of trends towards stagnation and protectionism in the centre and their effects on peripheral exports? What limits are there to a strategy of economic growth with external openness essentially grounded on expansion of consumption of imports, of the financial and services sectors, and of primary export activities? Has 1930 been forgotten?[4]

Before examining in greater depth the events of the early 1980s, we will return briefly to an analysis of the reasons for rapid expansion of the Euro-markets in the 1970s, and the impact of that expansion on developing countries, and on the nature of the international financial system.

The growth of the Euro-currency market, the growth of its lending to developing countries, and its impact

What were the main reasons private banking credits grew so rapidly that they became the most important single element in international capital movements in the 1970s? We shall attempt to describe briefly the different factors that contributed to this change, stressing the fact that the recycling of petrodollars since 1974 has only accelerated a pre-existent trend; we shall then attempt to explain the entrance of developing countries into the Euro-currency market. Finally, we shall stress some of the distortions introduced into the international financial system by the magnitude and modality of the growth of private bank lending in the 1970s.

Growth of Euro-markets

Since the 1960s, most of the world's major banks have emulated other large corporations by becoming multinational. They established branches and subsidiaries outside their national borders at an unprecedented rate. In 1960, eight US banks had foreign branches; by 1975, 125 US banks had foreign branches. Total assets of US overseas branches jumped from US $3.5 billion in 1960 to US $181 billion by June 1976. Other large countries' multinational banking growth started later, but at a very rapid state. Multinational banks' overseas operations were very concentrated. In 1976, thirteen US banks controlled over two-thirds of all US bank foreign activity; and the international earnings of these banks represented over 95 per cent of the increase in their total earnings between 1970 and 1975.[5]

It was natural that banks all over the world should have become multinational to meet the needs of their multinational corporate customers, who were increasingly investing and reinvesting their assets abroad. The general expansion of world trade after the Second World War was an additional demand factor influencing the growth of multinational banking. The role of the dollar as an international currency provided the base on which transnational banking developed.

Most analysts agree that this rapid growth of multinational banking is to a great extent attributable to the asymmetry between the stringent and detailed official regulations governing residents operating their own national currencies, and the great freedom of non-residents to operate in foreign currencies from the same constrained national banking system. (This would explain the fact that the transnationalization of finance has outstripped that of production, and that, since the early 1960s, the proportion of profits earned in foreign operations as compared with total profits of US transnational banks rose much faster than this same proportion for US transnational productive corporations.) As we shall see, the main centres of transnational banking have developed in countries where the least regulatory restriction was placed on their activity, and where more favourable tax treatment was granted.

In the late 1950s, two developments had allowed multinational banks to move into Europe. In 1958, Western Europe returned to full current account convertibility, particularly for non-residents. Authorized banks were allowed to take long and short positions in any currency. Increasing Soviet trade with the West generated dollars which the Soviet government preferred to deposit in Europe, to avoid a possible freeze by the US government.

A far stronger impulse towards transnational banking growth was given by several US government regulations, introduced in the 1960s to stem US foreign investment, in an attempt to improve the balance of payments. In 1964, the persistent US balance of payments deficit was in danger of increasing even more as a result of the over-heating of the American economy—caused by tax cuts—accompanied by increased military expenditure abroad— caused by the Vietnam War.

The Interest Equalization Tax was introduced on foreign stocks or debt obligations acquired by US individuals and corporations. It stimulated US multinational corporations to deposit their earnings abroad instead of repatriating them, and to finance new offshore investments through borrowing abroad by overseas affiliates; this trend was reinforced in 1968 by mandatory controls on capital exports of US multinationals. The 1965 Voluntary Foreign Credit Restraint Program curtailed short-term lending to non-residents located in the US, exempting from these ceilings their foreign branches and subsidiaries. US banks responded by shifting transactions from the home office to branches and subsidiaries abroad. Several Federal Reserve regulations encouraged US banks to hold foreign deposits offshore rather than in the US. Regulations put interest ceilings on time and saving deposits in US banks, again exempting offshore branches.

Even though many of these controls were terminated or diminished by 1974, they undoubtedly did much to expand offshore US banking. As one observer summarized: 'The American attempt to stop the export of capital in the nineteen sixties led to the export of the American banking system instead.'

The main centre of transnational banking activity has been—and to a lesser extent still is—London. The main reason for this is that, when transnational banking developed, London was one of the world's main financial centres. Its large size was linked basically to the absence of regulation over a long period; banks could accept deposits and make loans in any currency but sterling (since 1979 also in sterling) free of regulatory restraint, as no interest ceilings or reserve requirements are imposed. In addition, private banks had confidence in the Bank of England as a successful monetary authority with one and a half centuries of experience.

Other major centres are provided by a rapidly growing number of 'offshore havens', offering not only the absence of practically any form of banking regulation or oversight, but also strict banking secrecy and no taxation of foreign banks. Most banking transactions are still decided in the head offices of financial centres in the developed world. However, many are registered in the account of the bank's offshore branch (often in offices with little more than a nameplate on the door and a receptionist to answer the phone). These operations use a mechanism called the inter-bank market, which makes it easy for banks with a multinational base to minimize tax payments. The bank's 'booking procedures' can be compared with transfer pricing for other multinational corporations. In both cases, profit-taking is shifted from one sovereign tax jurisdiction to another, minimizing the corporation's worldwide burden—an operation simpler for the banks than for other multinationals. Finance capital flows more easily from one country to another than physical capital, under changing conditions. Multinational banks have little physical investment and relatively few skilled non-mobile personnel; they can shift their operations and subsidiaries from one country to another, so as to minimize tax payments, with greater ease and speed, and with smaller costs, than productive multinational corporations.

The multinational banking market specializing in borrowing and lending of currencies outside the country of issue is commonly known as the 'Euro-dollar market'. However, the term 'Euro-dollar' is not very accurate. This market is no longer limited to Europe—the Far East and the Caribbean have a substantial share of operations. Neither does it deal only in dollars, even though this is still the major currency. In fact, a term such as 'transnational currency market' would be more precise.

The main final borrowers in this market are national monetary authorities, state enterprises, multinational corporations, and official international organizations; however, most Euro-currency transactions are between banks. The majority of transactions are above US $1 million. This international capital market offers two different types of finance: large-scale credits and bonds. The main difference is that the latter have fixed interest rates, and are on the whole reserved for 'first-class borrowers'. Developing countries' participation as borrowers in the Euro-bond market during the 1970s was small and heavily concentrated (a high proportion of that participation was taken up by Mexico and Brazil). The share of developing countries in the Euro-bond market fell to 6 per cent in 1981, and declined even further afterwards.[6]

As can be seen in Table 6.3, the Euro-currency market has grown very rapidly and steadily since the mid-1960s. Its growth accelerated somewhat after the large rise in the price of oil (although the growth of the Euro-market was by no means solely a result of 'petro-dollar recycling', as some analysts have inaccurately claimed).

It is necessary to point out a problem of the BIS (Bank for International Settlements) series used here. Even though inter-bank deposits of foreign currencies are netted out for the industrialized countries, many inter-bank transactions are still included. This accepted measure of the Euro-currency market is not comparable to monetary aggregates at a national level, which

72   *Privatization of the Financial System in the 1970s*

Table 6.3. Size of the Euro-currency market, 1964–82

End of the year[a]	Net size of narrowly defined Euro-currency market[b] US $ billion
1964	12
1965	13
1966	16
1967	21
1968	20
1969	44
1970	57
1971	71
1972	92
1973	132
1974	177
1975	205
1976	247
1977	300
1978	375
1979	475
1980	575
1981	661
1982	686

Notes:
a. Refers to December for 1964–81, and to September for 1982.
b. Source: Bank for International Settlements (BIS), several *Annual Reports*, and *International Banking Developments—Third Quarter 1982*, Basle, December 1982. A problem of the BIS series is its 'parochial' European nature. Its advantage is the availability of consistent statistics since 1964; there is no alternative consistent series available which goes back to the 1960s.

Broader measures of foreign claims of banks (such as the IMF's IFS series) include, in addition to banks in industrial countries and offshore countries, the foreign claims of deposit money banks in many developing countries. In recent years, this measure has grown even faster than the figures in this table. For a good discussion of Euromarket figures, see IMF, 'International Capital Markets: Development and Prospects', Occasional Paper 14, Washington, DC, 1982.

measures only assets held by non-banks. In fact, attempts to eliminate completely inter-bank transactions from the Euro-currency market (and thus make it comparable to national macroeconomic aggregates) have necessarily failed, as the very essence of this market is linked to inter-bank transactions.

Increased lending to developing countries

At the same time as the Euro-currency market expanded at a very rapid pace, the proportion of its loans going to developing countries grew very substantially, reaching about 50 per cent in the late 1970s. These large flows have led to an increasing 'privatization' of the structure of the debt of developing countries.

We shall now examine briefly the factors which determined this rapid increase in Euro-currency lending to the developing countries, as well as the changes in the mechanisms within this market which have made access easier for them. We shall then study the evolution throughout the 1970s of the trends in developing countries' financing in the Euro-currency market.

Private multinational corporations and public borrowers of the industrial countries were the biggest users of the Euro-currency markets in the 1960s. As we saw, in this period, the external sources of finance for the developing countries were suppliers' credits and official flows (both bilateral and multilateral). In the late 1960s some countries—for example, Brazil and Mexico—began to obtain large loans from multinational private banks. This trend, which became more important between 1970 and 1973, reached particularly large dimensions after 1974.

Most analysts agree that the rapid rise in Euro-currency loans to the developing countries is not due to changed conditions in those countries so much as to developments and changes in the Euro-currency markets themselves. On the one hand, an increasing number of multinational banks were more and more keen to lend to the third world. Intense competition, and the search for new borrowers, seem to have been intensified by the rapid increase in the number of banks active in the Euro-markets. The Euro-banks' wish to diversify their portfolios geographically (and thus spread risks) was added to the relatively low growth of corporate credit demand in the developed countries. Very high rates of increase for commodity prices, and consequent improvements in the trade balance of the countries in the periphery during the early 1970s, made such countries attractive clients for these multinational bankers. Furthermore, multinational bankers had become acquainted with some of the peripheral countries during the 1960s and early 1970s, when providing finance to the branches of their multinational corporate clients, based in the periphery. The main factors in the growth of lending to developing countries was that, as the credit demand of traditional clients slowed down because of the recession in industrial countries, deposits from oil exporters and other sources were growing very fast. This prompted the banks to lend to borrowers previously considered marginal.

At the same time, there were factors which made both the public and the private sector in most of the developing countries keen to borrow. Governments were embarking on programmes of expanded public investment, which often contained a high proportion of imported capital goods, and often were not fully financed with the country's own resources. This was accompanied by relative stagnation in the net flow of official development assistance. There were also certain governmental attitudes in developing countries which tended to favour increased borrowing from private banking sources. Governments may have preferred private loans, as banks *seemed* to apply hardly any conditionality for disbursement of their loans. Loans could be made effective quickly and, formally, had few strings attached as to how funds were to be employed or how the country's economy should be managed. This was perceived as contrasting with the behaviour of international lending institutions or bilateral aid donors, which have traditionally applied a high degree of formal conditionality. It has been reported that several countries in the mid-1970s (for example, Colombia and Brazil) planned to seek independence in national economic planning and policy from the influence of bilateral and multilateral assistance institutions, by obtaining large commercial credits.[7] New financial options seemed to provide an additional range of manœuvre for governments in developing countries. Furthermore, in some developing countries, reliance on foreign direct investment was reduced as the governments expressed a policital preference for contractor, agency, or mixed-enterprise arrangements with foreign companies, which generally implied an increase in the demand for private foreign loans. The preference of governments often coincided with that of the transnational corporations themselves; mainly because of their desire to minimize risk, these corporations often preferred to reduce their equity investment and increase finance by loans. Thus, governments seemed to prefer private foreign loans both to official credits and to direct investment, partly because the former were perceived as generating a lesser degree of dependence, thus allowing greater autonomy for the national government.

The forces described above determined the willingness of multinational banks to lend to developing countries, as well as these countries' willingness to borrow. The development of new operational techniques in the Euro-currency market, particularly during the late 1960s, allowed a reduction in the individual risk for the Euro-banks making these loans to developing countries.

Several innovations occurred which seemed to diminish the risks for individual banks making large loans with long maturities—that is, the type of credits required by developing countries. First, the roll-over credit was created, based on a floating interest rate that varies approximately with the cost of the money for the lender, who obtains his funds on the essentially short-term inter-bank market. The base rate for these loans to the developing countries is often LIBOR (London Inter-Bank Offer Rate), or the US prime rate, which are measures of the cost of funds to the banks. In addition to this variable base rate, a 'spread' or margin over LIBOR or the US prime rate is charged; it reflects both the liquidity in the market at the time and creditworthiness of the borrower. The cost of the credit also includes a 'management fee', and a 'commitment fee', charged on the unused portion of funds. Thus, although the loan to the developing country may have a long maturity (for example, ten years), the interest rate is changed every time the credit is 'rolled-over' (usually every three or six months). This floating interest rate eliminated for banks the risk arising out of possible divergences between the rates of interest on their borrowed funds and those on their loans. One of the most important risks of the market (whose significance is discussed below) was transferred to the borrower, who had to bear both the cyclical and the long-term changes of interest rates.

Secondly, a very large part of the transactions on the Euro-currency markets by developing countries have been made through syndicated loans. Syndicated loans, which originated in the late 1960s, are credits shared by a larger number of Eurobanks. This mechanism has allowed the default risks of large loans to be spread over a great number of banks. It also allowed smaller banks to participate in the Euro-currency market, as they largely relied on the 'expertise' and experience in international lending of the lending banks.

Thirdly, the growth of a very large international inter-bank market was seen by banks to reduce funding risk, as it facilitated the adjustment of liquidity positions on both assets and liabilities.

The transnationalization of private bank lending, and its link to past flows

Again, as in the case of direct investment and official flows, multinational bank lending on a larger scale was initiated mainly by US institutions; after initial dominance by US banks, private lending became increasingly 'transnationalised'. This trend became much more marked in the second half of the 1970s; while, in December 1977, US banks accounted for about 50 per cent of total outstanding claims on all LDCs, the share of US banks' lending between December 1977 and June 1979 was less than 10 per cent.[8] As lending by US banks to the LDCs started to grow much more slowly (mainly because US banks were concerned at the high level of their LDC exposure), the initiative was taken by West European, Japanese, and OPEC banks.

As discussed above, in Latin America in the 1960s, net official inflows financed net outflows of foreign direct investment (as the latter flows were higher than the former). In the 1970s, an important and growing proportion of total private bank lending serviced payments of profit remittances by foreign investors, interest and amortization of official debt, and, increasingly, the private credits themselves. As can be seen ·in Table 6.4, the category of foreign investments' profits remained relatively constant as a proportion of exports of goods and services, while both interest payments and amortization soared, particularly from the mid-1970s onwards. This latter trend is due both to the 'privatisation' of the debt (which leads to shorter average maturities and an increase in the proportion of credits serviced on variable commercial interest rates) and to the dramatic rise of Euro-market interest rates since 1979.

Privatization of the Financial System in the 1970s 77

Table 6.4. Net financial service charges of Latin America, excluding oil exporters, relative to exports of goods and services (Percentages)

Period	Interests[a]	Profits[b]	Amortization[c]	Capital service ratio[d]
1950–4	1.3	5.9	2.8	10.0
1955–9	2.3	5.2	7.2	14.7
1960–4	4.0	6.5	10.9	21.4
1965–9	5.5	8.8	13.7	27.0
1970–3	7.4	7.1	17.2	31.9
1974–6	11.1	5.5	19.1	35.7
1977–9	12.0	6.8	28.1	47.0[e]

Source: E. Bacha and C. Diaz-Alejandro, 'Financial Markets: A View from the Periphery', paper presented at the International Seminar on External Financial Relations, Santiago de Chile, 19–21 March 1981.
*Notes*3:
a. Refers to net interest and profits (subtracting those received by Latin American residents.
b. This category over-estimates the impact on balance of payments, as it includes earning of foreign direct investment, whether remitted abroad or reinvested domestically.
c. Amortizations cover those for both private and public debt of more than one year.
d. Capital service ratio is the sum of the three former columns. The debt service ratio would be the sum of the first and the third columns.
e. Only 1977–8.

The impact of bank lending on developing countries and on the international financial system

As discussed above, the large volume of private lending helped *some* developing countries to sustain or even to increase levels of economic activity. Furthermore, it helped to sustain economic activity in the developed countries, by maintaining demand for their exports from the third world.

Private banks clearly preferred lending to countries with relatively high per capita income, as well as to those whose recent growth record was more impressive. Poor countries (in terms both of income levels and/or of natural resources) were not considered to be sufficiently 'creditworthy' to attract significant flows. As a result, private bank lending was concentrated to a very high degree among the upper- and middle-income developing countries. Low-income countries are estimated to have obtained only *2.6 per cent* of total net lending to oil-importing developing countries in the period 1972–80.[9] So the swing to private flows worsened the distribution of access to external finance among developing countries.

A second problem is presented by the financial conditions of the private loans. Compared with official loans, maturities of private loans are shorter. Of greater importance is that the cost of borrowing privately has been higher. Perhaps even more problematic is that the interest rate on much of private lending was variable, changing every three to six months as interest rates in the main industrial countries changed, especially those of the USA. This variability added an important element of uncertainty to borrowers' attempts to predict and plan their balance of payments flows. Price instability for developing countries' commodity exports, also became characteristic of the transfer of financial resources.

Floating interest costs varied significantly: the yearly average for deposit rates fluctuated between 5.5 per cent and 16.5 per cent between 1970 and 1981, with monthly averages varying even more, from 4.9 per cent (May 1972) to 19.9 per cent (March 1980). The average floating interest costs of developing countries, according to OECD estimates, more than doubled, from 8.2 per cent of outstanding debt in 1971–3 to 18.0 per cent in 1981. The effect of an increasing proportion of such variable interest debt in total borrowing, and significantly higher rates of interest, was to increase sharply the total cost of interest and total debt service, as a proportion of total debt and of exports. Furthermore, as reported in the World Bank 1981 *World Development Report*, the proportion of gross borrowing actually available for buying imports and increasing reserves—the net transfer—fell sharply— from 50 per cent in 1975–6 to 22 per cent in 1980. In fact, at the average debt terms available to Latin America in 1981, *gross lending would have had to double after six years and quadruple after ten years, merely to sustain a constant level of net transfer*.

More broadly, it can be argued that the changes in banking practices described above, designed to reduce important categories of risk for individual banks, often *de facto* increased risks arising from unfavourable changes affecting many borrowers simultaneously, such as the impact of a world recession—these are sometimes called systemic risks.[10]

For example, syndication of loans provides no protection against widespread decline in borrowers' ablity to service their debts caused by a deterioration in the international markets for goods or funds (or both). The variable interest rate implies that the interest rate risk is passed on to the borrower, which, if interest rates rise too much, implies that the interest rate risk for the lender is translated into increased credit risk. Furthermore, the inter-bank market—which facilitates funding under normal conditions —becomes a potential source of increased instability during periods of disturbance.

Both at a country level and for important categories of countries, private international lending is not stable, but often unpredictable, and varies in a pro-cyclical manner (this became particularly evident in the early 1980s, but should have been clear to anyone with at least a superficial knowledge of economic history). As Carlos Massad[11] succinctly put it: 'Interest rates, terms of trade and the supply of lending (can) interact perversely in the international transmission of disequilibria.' It was this negative, 'perverse' interaction between high levels of interest rates and a dramatic reduction in the supply of new private lending which led, in 1982–4, to the large net negative transfers of financial resources from Latin America described above.

As events in the early 1980s showed, the combination of an inadequate international financial system and a deep world recession not only deeply harmed growth and development in the third world, but also endangered the stability of the international private banking system itself.

Notes

1. We are referring here to the propositions, intentions, and measures incorporated in development policy, not to what was actually achieved.
2. Data based on IMF, *World Economic Outlook*, several issues.
3. C. F. Diaz-Alejandro, 'Latin American Debt: I Don't Think We Are in Kansas Anymore', *Brooking Papers on Economic Activity* 2, 1984.

4. See O. Sunkel, 'Comentarios sobre E. Bacha y C. Diaz-Alejandro; "Mercados Financieros: Una Vision desde la Semiperiferia"', in R. Ffrench-Davis, ed., *Las Relaciones Financieras Externas, su Efecto en la Economia Latinoamericana*, Mexico, Fondo de Cultura Economica, Serie Lecturas 47, 1983, p. 69. The foregoing pages arc a revised version of this article.

5. US Congress, Senate Committee on Foreign Relations, *International Debt: The Banks and US Foreign Policy*, prepared by Karin Lissakers, 95th Congress, 1st session, Washington, DC, 1977, pp. 9–12.

6. C. Johnson, 'What Are the Prospects for Growth in International Credit Markes?', paper presented to *Financial Times / Banker's World Banking Conference*, 9 December 1982.

7. P. A. Wellons, *Borrowing by Developing Countries on the Euro-Currency Market*, Paris, 1977; S. Dell and R. Lawrence, *The Balance of Payments Adjustment Process in Developing Countries*, New York, 1980.

8. E. Bacha and C. Diaz-Alejandro, 'Financial Markets: A View from the Periphery', paper presented at the International Seminar on External Financial Relations, Santiago de Chile, 19–21 March 1981.

9. See, for example, sources with such different analytical frameworks as US Congress Committee on Foreign Relations, *International Debt*; R. E. McKinnon, 'The Euro-currency Market', *Essays in International Finance* 125, Princeton, December 1977; and J. D. Aronson, *Money and Power*, Beverly Hills and London, 1977.

10. See, for example, UNCTAD, *Trade and Development Report*, UNCTAD /TDR/4, vol. 2, July 1984.

11. C. Massad, 'Implications of the External Debt for International Finance', *Development* 1, 1984.

CHAPTER 7

The Slow-down of Growth in the Industrial Countries

The weaknesses of the system of international financial inter-mediation existing in the late 1970s meant that the industrial countries' recession of the early 1980s provoked both an inter-national debt crisis and a crisis of national development, particularly (but not only) in Latin American countries.

In the next two chapters we will first (Chapter 8) examine how the recession in industrial countries played a major role in sparking off widespread debt crises in Latin America, and in the rest of the developing world; then (Chapter 9) we will analyse why the industrial countries' recovery in the mid-1980s seems to be of a magnitude and nature such that it will not allow both the debt crises and the crises of national development to be simultaneously overcome, as a large number of optimistic observers were forecasting in late 1984 and early 1985.

Before turning to those concerns, we will explore the nature of the recession that occurred in the industrial countries in the 1980s. Basically, two different hypotheses were advanced to interpret the recession. The first maintains that it was just a recession, somewhat more protracted than usual, in which, unfortunately, several coincident negative factors have combined to produce particularly severe effects in Latin America, but that, particularly in 1984, there was an important recovery in the USA; the proper response is to be patient, and 'adjust' until the positive effects of recovery begin to make themselves felt, for then will come a new phase of expansion that will alleviate the acute problems of today.

Another very different view sees this recession as a deep-seated structural problem, in which the recession and accompanying financial problems are only symptoms which may easily be confused with a transient recession, but behind which in reality lie profound and immensely far-reaching, long-term problems, whose outcome cannot be forecast with any certainty, but which imply that future growth in the industrial countries will be significantly slower than it was in the exceptional period after the Second World War, and that this growth is likely to have less beneficial effects on developing countries than that which occurred in the post-war period.

It is essential to take a position *vis-à-vis* these alternatives. In the first case, the appropriate strategy is to ride out the storm until it dies down, and to go ahead with the traditional development strategies. In the second case, it is a matter of understanding that there is no such passing storm, but the tempestuous close of a particularly expansionist epoch or phase of capitalism, and that an attempt must be made to advance by new routes, learning from the lessons of the past, but not turning back, exploring new future options—and all this in a turbulent and difficult international context, very different from that prevailing in the first two decades after the war. This is the alternative towards which the authors of the present study incline, for reasons that we will try to develop more fully in what follows.

In our exploration of this field we shall seek the company of several authorities, seeing to it that they represent a broad ideological spectrum. According to Paul Samuelson, Nobel Prize-winner in Economics, whose position is well in the centre of the doctrinal gamut, no one can confidently predict the future; but, after careful consideration, he thinks that the last quarter of the twentieth century will show a rate of economic progress far below that attained in the third quarter.[1]

Within the Marxist tradition, one of its most outstanding representatives, Professor Ernest Mandel, by the early 1970s already saw in the 1974–5 recession one of the recurrent crises of the capitalist system, characterized since the mid-1960s by a decline in the profitability of enterprises as a consequence of a twofold process of over-accumulation of capital and under-consumption. The boom phase of the lengthy cycle which the system is experiencing at present would seem to have come to an end in 1967, when a long recessive phase began.[2]

The third quotation, from a conservative standpoint, comes from the BIS 1983 Annual Report.

The process of disinflation upon which the Western industrial world had embarked in the wake of the second oil crisis . . . has been accompanied, at least until recently, by stagnation of output in the industrial world as a whole. It is probable that the wrong policy mix, i.e., the excessive burden borne by monetary policy in imposing global restraint, made the stagnation more protracted than it would otherwise have been. And it is certain that by exerting upward pressure on interest rates the policy mix had a particularly inhibiting influence on capital formation, thus mortgaging future growth potential. But one should not forget that the Western industrial countries' growth problems did not begin three years ago, when they jointly undertook to resist the cost-push of the second oil shock. The first signs of a break in growth trends, at least as far as fixed capital investment is concerned, were evident in the late 1960s and early 1970s, well before the first oil shock. The deeper-seated causes of the break remain uncertain, but the more immediate ones are not: the rising share of labour in income distribution, the declining profitability of businesses, the expanding role of the public sector, sluggish capital formation and weakening productivity growth.

Nor should one attribute the current level of unemployment exclusively to the demand-restraining policies of the last three years. Unemployment, particularly in Western Europe, was on an upward trend well before that, under the combined influence of slower growth, an expanding population and in some countries increases in the labour-force participation rates. Last but not least, the excessive rise in real wage costs and growing impediments to labour mobility gave a major incentive to labour-saving investment and innovations. It is against this background that the recent declines in real wages, beyond their direct contributions to slowing inflation, are a helpful element of adjustment.[3]

The exceptional post-war boom began to fade out by the end of the 1960s (see Table 7.1). In all the industrialized countries, productivity increased from the mid-1950s to the mid-1960s. This trend was reversed in almost all cases in the second half of the 1960s, after which a slight recovery was shown in some countries in the early 1970s, to be followed in the rest of the decade by a slump. This decline in productivity towards the end of the 1960s was also reflected in such indicators as the profitability of enterprises, the decrease in the rate of capital formation, and the increase in unemployment. Most of the analyses of the period, which are based on trends in gross product and in foreign trade, overlook that essential turning-point, since those indicators, after a reduction in the years 1970 and 1971, made a vigorous recovery in 1972 and 1973. Accordingly, many analysts of the crisis take 1973 as a major milestone, which in our opinion introduces a serious bias into the analysis, by attributing the end of the post-war era of expansion implicitly and often explicitly almost exclusively to the oil crisis.

Table 7.1. The growth of labour productivity in selected OECD countries, 1955–80 (Percentages)

Country	Total economy				
	Late 1950s	Early 1960s	Late 1960s	Early 1970s	Late 1970s
USA	1.8	3.0	1.0	1.4	0.3
Canada	1.7	2.5	2.0	2.8	0.2
UK	2.2	3.1	2.8	3.1	1.1
Sweden	n.a.	4.5	3.1	2.0	0.4
Denmark	5.2	3.7	3.3	2.8	1.3
Norway	3.8	4.5	3.5	1.5	2.5
Finland	3.6	4.7	5.1	4.7	2.5
Netherlands	4.0	3.1	4.4	4.4	1.9
Belgium	2.5	5.2	3.9	4.4	2.4
Germany	4.6	4.9	4.6	4.1	3.2
Austria	5.0	4.6	6.4	5.2	2.8
France	4.3	5.0	4.5	4.7	2.9
Italy	4.6	5.0	6.2	4.2	1.7
Japan	8.4	12.5	8.6	6.3	3.0

Source: Herbert Giersch and Frank Wolter, 'Towards an Explanation of the Productivity Slowdown: An Acceleration–Deceleration Hypothesis', *Economic Journal* 93, March 1983, Table 1, p. 36.

The fact that the process of stagnation had begun by the mid-1960s is thus lost to view.[4]

In order to see this phenomenon in a clearer light, it should be fitted into a broader historical framework (see Table 7.2). This throws into relief something which economists had forgotten, or which, with their characteristic arrogance, they thought had been overcome by the progress and perfecting of economic policy; the irregular, cyclical nature of capitalist development, not only over the short and medium but also over the long term. It can be seen that, from the beginning of the nineteenth century to our own time, capitalist development has passed through several protracted phases of expansion and stagnation of production, per capita income, productive fixed capital formation, and exports (see Table 7.2).

The first phase of expansion lasted almost a century, up to 1913;

then supervened a long wave of recession between 1913 and 1950; next followed a new and very marked expansionist cycle, between 1950 and 1973; and later still, between 1973 and 1979, came the dawn of what would appear to be a new and long-drawn-out phase of recession. This last period, as argued above, really began several years before, and the last few years should also be added, making up a period of about fifteen years of relative stagnation. It is not surprising, therefore, that there should have been a revival of Kondratieff's theory of long waves of cycles.[5] Does this last period really constitute the beginning of a lengthy phase of stagnation, or is it merely a matter of taking a deep breath, or heaving several profound sighs, before resuming the noteworthy rate of expansion characteristic of the period following the war? To decide this point, it is necessary to examine the nature of that extraordinary phase of expansion, and to see whether the conditions on which it was based still exist or have disappeared. To that end, we shall examine some aspects of the evolution of the primary factors of production (human, natural, capital, and energy), of the state of the productive forces and their technological

Table 7.2. Growth characteristics of different phases, 1820–1979 (Arithmetical average of figures for the individual countries)

Phases	(Annual average compound growth rates)			
	GDP	GDP per head of population	Tangible reproducible non-residential fixed capital stock	Volume of exports
I 1820–70	2.2^a	1.0^b	...	4.0^a
1870–1913	2.5	1.4	2.9	3.9
II 1913–50	1.9	1.2	1.7	1.0
III 1950–73	4.9	3.8	5.5	8.6
IV 1973–9	2.5	2.0	4.4^c	4.8

Source: Angus Maddison, *Phases of Capitalist Development*, Oxford and New York, 1982, p. 91.
Notes:
a. Average for 13 countries.
b. Average for 10 countries.
c. 1973.

base, and of the national sociopolitical organization and its international context.

As regards productive resources, it should be recalled that the labour force has increased significantly in the developed countries, as a result of the population explosion recorded in the USA after the Second World War, and the immigration into Europe, especially into West Germany, of the displaced population of the countries of Eastern Europe. Subsequently, this manpower contingent went on expanding in the North Atlantic economy in consequence of immigration from the European and United States periphery, the *Gastarbeiter* phenomenon in Europe, and the quotas of Mexican, Central American, and Caribbean immigrants in the United States.

With respect to raw materials, investment in mineral, energy, and agricultural resources was rapidly renewed after the Second World War in view of the prospects of expansion of demand by the USA and, later on, by Europe and Japan, both for the purposes of reconstruction of these economies and to supply the demand deriving from the Cold War, and from hostilities such as those in Korea and other subsequent conflicts. A factor of importance in facilitating this investment was the gradual dismantling of the European colonial empires in Asia, Africa, and the Caribbean, which opened up these countries to US, German, and Japanese investment.

Where capital infrastructure was concerned, the US economy had not succeeded in fully utilizing its accumulated productive capacity until the last stage of the Second World War. And this tempo of activity was not recovered until the end of the 1940s.

This incorporation of relatively idle factors of production into the economic process was possible thanks to an exceptional expansion of global demand. It was manifested mainly in the resumption of military expenditure on rearmament in consequence of the start of the Cold War as from 1948, the Point IV programme to support the development of the less developed countries, the Marshall Plan for the reconstruction of the European countries devastated by the war, the creation of the European Common Market, the introduction of a set of redistribution and full employment policies, as part of the conception of the welfare state in the Eurorean countries, and the generalization of the US lifestyle and consumption patterns in the European countries and

Japan at first, and later among the privileged sectors in the rest of the world.

The logistic support for the establishment of the political, military, and economic hegemony of the USA was, moreover, one of the chief sources of the extension of the great US oligopolist corporations to the rest of the developed and underdeveloped world—or, in other words, one of the bases on which the transnational enterprise was able to expand at world level until, in time, it contributed to the generation of the transnational system.

The sustained expansion of demand, and of internal and international markets, the utilization of accumulated production capacity, and the enlargement of scales of production in the big multinational corporations, the introduction of technological innovations deriving from the Second World War and from the nuclear and space race of the post-war decades, together with the mass adoption of US vanguard technology in the European and Japanese economies, made possible a striking increase in capital formation, radical changes in the structure of production, economies of scale, agglomeration, and conglomeration, and improvements in productive efficiency, with a marked upswing in the productivity of labour. Behind all this a major contributing factor was the low price and gradually increasing cheapness of petroleum, the source of energy which came to be predominant in the post-war economy. This new energy base, in process of expansion, facilitated the increase in labour productivity by promoting the rapid and mass substitution of capital equipment for manpower. This was reflected, furthermore, in greater dynamism in those sectors of the economy that were most directly linked to the utilization of so exceptionally versatile and cheap a source of energy: the motor vehicle industry, the metal-working and electronics industries producing durable consumer goods, the petrochemical industry, and the artificialization of agriculture (mechanization, chemical inputs, artificial climate, and conservation).

This combination of factors was favourable to a highly oligopolized economic structure, in which the dynamics of competition between the great transnational corporations was increasingly channelled into rapid innovations in technology and design, differentiation of output, and inordinate promotion of consumption and manipulation of the consumer, through scientific publicity and sales techniques as well as the almost unlimited extension of consumer credits: all this based on a veritable revolution in communications.[6] The levels and patterns of consumption of individuals, families, and society as a whole became their central social objectives and values, determining their social status within the national framework and in the international system. The demonstration effect came to be the lodestar of social aspirations both among countries and among the social classes within countries, and the development criterion and ideology of national growth and 'modernization', taking this to mean the assimilation and reproduction of the behaviour patterns, values, consumption, technology, social, and even institutional and political organization characteristic of the industrialized countries and in particular of the USA.

In the case of Latin America, this interpretation of development policy took formal shape in the Alliance for Progress (see Chapter 5). The idea, in essence, was to promote economic growth by means of major transport, communications, and energy infrastructure projects, in order to facilitate industrial development, the modernization of agriculture (including its institutional transformation through agrarian reform), and urbanization, which, together with the expansion of general and higher education, were aimed at building up large urban middle classes; these, by sharing the life-style, consumer patterns, and values of the developed world, would be the pillars of an economic development of capitalist character under a democratic political system, closely linked to the North Atlantic alliance.

As has been noted, the exceptional dynamism of this economic growth style of the industrialized countries began to slacken at the end of the 1960s. The reasons are of various kinds. In the first place, during the period analysed, and especially in its early phases, there were certain initial conditions and factors and unique phenomena that were irreproducible—such as the existence of idle capacity in the US economy, European reconstruction, the integration of Europe, industrial and agricultural modernization, especially in Europe and Japan, and the liberalization of international trade—all of which helped to stimulate expansion but, once their possibilities were exhausted, disappeared from the scene.

Another group of factors served as driving forces up to a point, but in so far as their use was extended beyond certain limits they changed from positive to negative, and began to turn into constraints on expansion. Cases in point were the increasing costs for the state of financing gigantic military set-ups and performing income redistribution and social welfare functions, and the rise in the real cost of labour deriving from full employment policies and the strengthening of the trade unions' bargaining power. These were at first factors making for the expansion of demand, but when certain levels were exceeded they resulted in a reduction of the profitability of enterprises and in inflationary pressures, either on account of the fiscal deficit or because of increased taxation.

The expansion of foreign investment through the transnational corporations also enjoyed an extremely dynamic and positive phase, but the time came when high real costs of labour, heavy taxation, and environmental protection requirements meant that the profitability of the subsidiaries surpassed that of the parent firms. These latter began to transfer their operations *en masse* to other countries, developed, underdeveloped, and even socialist, not only to broaden their markets, but, what was more, to re-export from them to their countries of origin, ousting traditional activities, and generating unemployment problems in the process.[7]

Another phenomenon of this type is the rapid reconstruction, modernization, and exceptional dynamism of the European and Japanese economies, which at first contributed to the economic expansion of the industrialized centre, but which, as time went by, began to cause friction amongst the countries forming it with the intensification of competition amongst the European countries, between these and the USA, and between Japan and all the rest. Trade deficits were thus generated in the less competitive countries, which adopted restrictive and protectionist policies—thereby cramping not only their own expansion, but also that of the more dynamic countries, indirectly, that of the less developed countries, and, in the last analysis, that of the entire world economy.

A similar case was that of the developing countries which diversified and expanded their exports of non-traditional items and manufactures and began to gain a foothold in the markets of the industrial countries; in so far as they multiplied, grew, and were successful, they created problems for equivalent activities in the industrial countries, which provoked the corresponding protectionist reaction.

The increasing US trade deficit generated by these differential trends in productivity and international competition, and aggravated by military, external aid, and foreign investment commitments, and by such events as the hostilities in Vietnam, finally led to the relinquishment of the dollar/gold standard in August 1971. This marked the collapse of the system of international economic institutions established at Bretton Woods, with the dollar as a reserve currency.

As the vulnerability of the dollar became increasingly patent, a number of speculative manœuvres against the existing parities were initiated, facilitated by the elimination of exchange controls in Europe and the rapid expansion of the Euro-currencies market, in which it was easy to obtain credit for speculative purposes. The agreement reached in December 1971 on the management of exchange adjustments was annulled in 1973, inasmuch as fixed parities were no longer possible in face of the creation of an international financial market which facilitated speculation. Once again an expansionist process of trade and financial liberalization took place, which in a world of fixed and foreseeable parities had facilitated international trade and investment during a given period, but which, in face of growing real imbalances amongst the member countries and the re-creation and vast expansion of an uncontrollable transnational private financial market, fell prey to speculative instability. The introduction of fluctuating exchange rates brought permanent instability into the system, and with it uncertainty and extreme caution in respect of productive investment, especially of a long-term character.

The energy crisis might be regarded as an exogenous shock which had an impact on the situation at two key points of time: 1973–4 and 1979. But, from a longer-term standpoint, we have been formulating the hypothesis that this was one of those virtuous circles which become vicious circles in the course of time. Because of the USA's exceptional resource endowments and its relative shortage of manpower, it had tended ever since the last century to adopt capital-intensive technologies. The plentifulness of oil resources, and the price and other advantages of this fuel, encouraged its widespread use and dissemination in the motor vehicle and petrochemical industries, and in the manufacture of electrical household appliances. Hence was engendered the development style described above, based, *inter alia*, on intensive utilization of this source of energy and, in general, of all the natural resources and environmental conditions which were exceptionally abundant in the USA. With the transnationalization process this style was generalized throughout the world, whereby demand for petroleum expanded to an inordinate extent and became increasingly inelastic as it was, to a greater or less extent, incorporated in patterns of technology, of production, of consumption, of territorial organization, and of human settlements in all countries, including those lacking in oil.[8] Thus it was that the petroleum-exporting countries realized that specific geopolitical circumstances had been created which allowed them to form a cartel and fix prices at a much higher level.

Whatever the interpretation of this phenomenon, its effects on the international economy have been of the greatest importance. In the first place, it caused a structural cost-inflation effect on account of the restriction of supplies of a basic input; secondly, it rendered obsolete a considerable proportion of the fixed capital structures whose operation depended upon petroleum, with consequent capital losses; and in addition it considerably enlarged the current account deficits of the petroleum-importing countries. At the same time, it contributed to the formation of the transnational banking system and the infusion of a formidable mass of liquidity of some US $2,000 billion into the international economic system during the past decade. This was a means of preventing an even worse recession, but it helped to generate very strong additional inflationary pressures, especially as a result of the 1979 oil crisis. Hence a new direction was given to economic policy: the economic growth and full employment targets adopted after the Second World War were abandoned, and every effort was concentrated on counteracting inflation and restoring basic systemic equilibria through a monetarist purge.[9]

Economic stagnation and growing unemployment, increasingly intensive inflationary pressures, and the contradictions deriving from a succession of short-term policies designed to 'warm up' and 'cool down' the economy time and again, were reflected in greater social tensions, and subsequently led to the breakdown of the coalition between capital, the middle-income sectors, and labour which was the political corner-stone of the welfare state, and of the Keynesian policies of full employment and expansion of consumption that characterized the prolonged post-war boom. What was possible in a period of expansion, when the struggle for redistribution was taking place in a situation in which everyone could gain, became impossible in a situation of stagnation, when the gains of some were obtained at the expense of the rest. It seems that this fundamental political fact—the disruption of a broad social and political consensus which extended from organized labour to the entrepreneurial sectors, and included the large middle-class strata of professionals, technicians, and employees of public and private bureaucracy—is what lies behind the resurgence of a highly reactionary position on the political right wing (and of a thorough-going revolutionary one on the left).

The reactionary position has two major manifestations: the use of the monetarist model as a macroeconomic explanation and, more essential still, the philosophico-ideological return to the classic traditions of Adam Smith's capitalism—that is, a radical revaluation of individualism. Society is not made up of social aggregates—classes, groups—but of individuals; everything can and must be interpreted in supply, demand, and market terms, be it law, the state, society, family life, or marriage; to everything can and must be applied the economic cost–benefit analysis. All this comes to constitute an ideology, a political programme, in which an attempt is made to dismantle the state apparatus as far as possible. The welfare state system is severely pruned because it interferes with each individual's decision as to what he must do with his income; state intervention in respect of investment is also restricted; and the weight carried by the state in terms of taxation and in particular of income tax is reduced in order to demolish a system which deprives the individual of incentives.[10]

Other necessary steps are to destroy or weaken the trade union organizations in order to forestall artificial interference in the labour market; to attempt to strip the state of all enterprises and activities that can be privatized; and, of course, not only to apply the principle of *laissez-faire* in internal affairs, but also to promote total openness of the national economy to the world economy, so that the domestic price system is regulated by the international price system to ensure that static comparative advantages determine resource allocation.

In macroeconomic terms, the growing influence of monetarist thinking and the rise in inflation in industrial countries during the 1970s meant that, increasingly from the mid-1970s, the medium-term strategy adopted by industrial countries was based on the assumption that effective control of inflation was a prerequisite for the attainment of higher levels of economic activity.[11] The extreme priority given to the fight against inflation, and the use of mainly macroeconomic policies—focused to a very large extent on restrictive monetary policies—began to increase in 1979. Thus the powerful Interim Committee of the IMF has repeatedly emphasized since 1979 that 'the main task of economic policy was to contain inflationary pressures and to reduce inflationary expectations'.

Even though there were important underlying structural causes for slow growth in the industrial countries (which we have attempted to outline in this chapter), the 1980–3 recession in the industrial countries (see Table 7.3) was exacerbated and prolonged by deliberate government policies in industrial countries whose main aim was clearly not growth or full employment in the short-term, but control of inflation.

Table 7.3. Growth of world output and trade, 1978–84 (Percentages)

	1978	1979	1980	1981	1982	1983	1984
Industrial countries' GDP	4.0	3.1	1.2	1.5	−0.2	2.0	4.0
Developing countries' GDP	4.1	5.0	3.2	1.6	0.5	0.0	3.5
World imports	5.5	5.2	1.2	1.6	−0.7	0.6	4.0

Source: UN *World Economic Survey*, E/1984/62, New York, 1984.

This attempt to interpret the evolution of the international economy after the Second World War would seem to suggest that the phase of dynamic expansion had come to an end by 1970, as a result of the disappearance, exhaustion, and reversal of a number of long-term forces, which were in operation during the period in question and since then have not been replaced. During the 1970s the political and energy bases that supported the development style in question collapsed, and a concept of economic policy directed towards growth and full employment was replaced by another, centred on monetary and financial stability at both national and international levels. Thus a period of serious instability, uncertainty, and confusion was generated in both national and international economic policies, culminating in

1980-3 in an acute and prolonged recession, superimposed upon the long-term structural crisis of the post-war development style.

Notes

1. Paul Samuelson, 'The World Economy at Century's End', *Japan Economic Journal*, 10 March 1983.
2. See Ernest Mandel, *Late Capitalism*, London, 1975; *The Second Slump: A Marxist Analysis of Recession in the Seventies*, London, 1978.
3. BIS, *Fifty-third Annual Report*, pp. 3-4.
4. This phenomenon is well documented. See H. Giersch and F. Wolter, 'Towards an Explanation of the Productivity Slowdown: An Acceleration-Deceleration Hypothesis'; A. Lindbeck, 'The Recent Slowdown of Productivity Growth'; and E. F. Denison, 'The Interruption of Productivity Growth in the United States', all in *Economic Journal* 93, March 1983. See also D. M. Leipziger, 'Productivity in the United States and its International Implications', *The World Economy* 3(1), June 1980; T. P. Hill, *Profits and Rates of Return*, Paris, 1979; S. Rosenberg and T. E. Weisskopf, 'A Conflict Theory Approach to Inflation in the Postwar US Economy', *American Economic Review* 71(2), 1981; OECD, *Economic Outlook*, December 1978.
5. See, for example, Angus Maddison, *Phases of Capitalist Development*, Oxford and New York, 1982; W. W. Rostov, 'Kondratieff, Schumpeter and Kuznets: Trend Periods Revisited', *Journal of Economic History*, December 1975, and his book, *The World Economy*, London, 1978. See also Mandel, *Late Capitalism* and *The Second Slump*, and the special number of *Futures* 13(4), August 1981, on 'Technical Innovation and Long Waves in World Economic Development', ed. Christopher Freeman.
6. See F. M. Scherer, *Industrial Market Structure and Economic Performance*, Chicago, 1971.
7. See F. Frobel, J. Heinricks, and O. Kreye, *Die neuve internationale Arbeitsteilung*, Reinbek bei Hamburg, 1977.
8. The hypothesis can be applied, with the appropriate reservations, to other non-renewable as well as to renewable natural resources, and particularly to certain ecosystems of critical significance for human survival in specific localities. This subject has been explored in recent years by the Joint ECLA/UNEP Development and Environment Unit in a number of studies: O. Sunkel, 'The Interaction Between Styles of Development and the Environment in Latin America', *CEPAL Review*, no. 12, December 1980; *Estilos de Desarrollo y*

Medio Ambiente en la America Latina, selection by O. Sunkel and N. Gligo, Series Lecturas no. 36, Mexico, Fondo de Cultura Economica, 1980; O. Sunkel, *La Dimension Ambiental en los Estilos de Desarrollo de America Latina*, E/CEPAL/G.1143, Santiago, ECLA/UNEP, 1981; N. Gligo, 'Estilos de Desarrollo, Modernizacion y Medio Ambiente en la Agricultura Latinoamericana', *Estudios e Informes de la CEPAL* no. 11, E/CEPAL/G.1196, Santiago, ECLA/UNEP, 1982; 'Informe de Seminario Regional sobre Metropolizacion y Medio Ambiente', E/CEPAL/L.266, Santiago, 1982; 'Estilos de Desarrollo, Energia y Medio Ambiente: Un Estudio de Caso Exploratorio', *Estudios e Informes de la CEPAL* no. 28, E/CEPAL/ G.1254, Santiago, ECLA/UNEP, July 1983; *Expansion de la Frontera Agropecuaria y Medio Ambiente en America Latina*, CEPAL/CIFCA, Madrid, 1983; 'Sobrevivencia Campesina en Ecosistemas de Altura', E/CEPAL/G.1267, Santiago, 1983.

9. BIS, *Fifty-third Annual Report*.

10. A good summary, with neoliberal leanings, is to be found in H. Lapage, *Mañana, el Capitalismo*, Santiago de Chile, 1979. See also P. Dews, 'The *nouvelle philosophie* and Foucault', *Economy and Society* 8(2), May 1979, in relation to the critique of the welfare state.

11. See, for example, OECD communiqué on meeting of Council at ministerial level in June 1976, *Activities of OECD in 1976, report by the Secretary General*, Paris, 1977.

CHAPTER 8

Causes and Management of Debt Crises in the early 1980s

'External' causes of the Latin American crises in the early 1980s

Much of the debate about the causes of the Latin American development and debt crises in the early 1980s centres on the extent to which external or internal causes provide the dominant explanation. This type of debate is important because it has implications for the design of future development strategies and for the discussions on the need and nature of international monetary reform. Furthermore, it is of significance for the more immediate discussion on how the cost of the debt burden should be shared.

It seems incorrect to us, however, to attempt too sharp a distinction between external and internal factors or forces. Precisely because such important sections of the Latin American economies and societies had become either integrated or intimately linked to the international economy (or 'transnationalized'), such a sharp analytical distinction does not seem to us to correspond any more to reality.

This problem seems well illustrated by the issue of capital flight, which we believe is an important contributory factor to explaining the crisis both of Latin American debt and of development. Several authors attribute capital flight to causes of an internal nature. For example, in an otherwise very perceptive commentary, Jeffrey Sachs[1] explicitly attributes the large volumes of capital flight from Latin America (which we will discuss below) to 'domestic policy mistakes'. Although domestic policies (such as overvalued exchange rates) clearly play a role in encouraging capital flight, so do the attitudes taken by private and public actors in the OECD countries, for example, in defending the secrecy of foreign bank accounts and of US treasury bond holders; undoubtedly very high real US interest rates have provided an additional incentive for capital flight. Furthermore, 'transnationalized citizens' indulging in capital flight are difficult to control by governments who have been deprived (or rather have deprived themselves) of instruments such as exchange controls that, however imperfectly, would allow them to curb such flows. As Diaz-Alejandro[2] clearly puts it,

internationalized households can overcome the uncertainties of under-development and erratic government . . . Increasingly, the international system offers Latin American middle and upper classes comfortable possibilities for capital and personal exit, decreasing their incentives for expressing their voice in local affairs and eroding their loyalty to the state, which nevertheless is expected by the OECD countries to collect taxes to service debt and to provide a suitable climate for investment, trade and governance.

The transnationalization of production and consumption patterns was accompanied in the late 1970s and early 1980s by a sharp increase in the transnationalization of private wealth and assets!

The fact that the crises both of debt and of development affected practically all the Latin American countries in the early 1980s does indeed point to the fact that externally determined elements played a major role in causing those crises. It was, however, the interaction between unfavourable and unstable circumstances in the international environment and the development strategies and policies that Latin American governments had been pursuing for some time which made these crises significantly larger. As a result, even though the crises may have a common origin, their internal effects have been either attenuated or aggravated by the countries' own characteristics, their previous development strategies, and their policies for dealing with external problems. The evidence seems to point to the fact that the major declines in output, income, and employment in Latin America tended to be larger in the countries (such as those of the Southern Cone) which had opened up their economies relatively far more to capital and trade flows, as well as trying to rely almost exclusively on the 'magic of the market' domestically. Furthermore, it is interesting that the Asian middle-income countries, which on the whole follow pragmatic policies of targeted state intervention and selective regulation of international trade and capital flows, weathered the crises of the early 1980s relatively far more successfully than their Latin American counterparts, in terms both of sustained growth and of far fewer debt crises. (It seems true, however, that some

Latin American countries were at a disadvantage because of the 'regionalization' syndrome affecting banks, and were to an important extent considered less creditworthy just because of their geographical location.)

The external factors contributing to the Latin American crises are linked to the severity of the recession that occurred in the industrial countries between 1980 and 1982, the policy mix used by industrial governments to secure disinflation, and the peculiar characteristics of the system of international financial intermediation (which we have discussed in previous chapters). Thus, while the disturbances transmitted from industrial to developing countries originated in the policy stance of the industrial countries, the transmission was greatly amplified by certain basic characteristics of the trade—and particularly the financial—system.

Industrial countries' rapid growth—which had begun in the early 1950s—started to slow down in the early 1970s for a number of structural reasons which we discussed in the previous chapter. In the late 1970s, overall macroeconomic policy in industrial countries was greatly tightened (particularly after the second large increase in the price of oil) to achieve 'disinflation', with a heavy reliance on monetary policy to pursue this target; thus there occurred simultaneously in the late 1970s sharp shifts both in the overall policy stance (more deflationary) and in the mix (far greater emphasis on monetary policy) in industrial countries.

A number of factors amplified the impact of the resulting recession on developing countries.

1. First, the value of commodity exports fell sharply, with decreases in prices being accompanied by proportionally smaller rises, or declines, in volume. As has been argued in the 1984 UNCTAD *Trade and Development Report*, such price 'flexibility', reflecting the effect of the short-term inelasticity in supply characterizing markets for primary commodities, aggravates the impact of world deflation. By the end of 1982, the UNCTAD index of market prices of the principal commodity exports of developing countries fell by one-third from its 1980 level, in terms of dollars, while in 'real' prices (that is, in terms of prices of manufactured goods) it declined by one-quarter during those two years.[3] For Latin American economies, it has been estimated that the terms of trade in 1983 were at a level 26 per cent lower than that in 1978.[4]

Clearly, the most important cause of the collapse of commodity prices in 1980–2 was the recession in the industrial countries. In addition, abnormally high interest rates—resulting from the policy mix with which disinflation was pursued—greatly increased the cost of holding commodity stocks, resulting in a large reduction of inventories which further reduced demand for a wide range of commodities. A number of supply-side factors further accentuated the price decline.[5] It would seem, furthermore, that more long-term structural factors operating in the economies of commodity-importing countries accentuated the impact of the recession on commodity prices; such structural factors include income support for domestic farmers in industrial countries, secular shift in patterns of food consumption as well as a slow-down in its total growth, and technological changes in the industrial sector which replace natural materials by synthetics.

2. A second factor which amplified the impact of the recession on developing countries in general, and on Latin American ones in particular, was the sharp escalation of interest rates, which increased dramatically the cost of these countries' accumulated debt, a high proportion of which had been contracted at variable interest rates. Latin America's gross remittances for interest payments rose at a spectacular rate, from around US $6.9 billion in 1977 to over US $39 billion in 1982. The impact of an increase of this magnitude on the balance of payments is clearly illustrated by the proportion of the region's current account deficit (see Table 8.1), which was attributable to net payments of interest and profits; this ratio, which in 1975 reached approximately 42 per cent, rose to 75 per cent in 1981, to somewhat over 100 per cent in 1982, and to an unprecedented 400 per cent in 1983! (In the last year, the increase in the ratio is due to the sharp decline in the current account deficit.)

As pointed out in Chapter 6, by the late 1970s debt had become an additional and new channel for the transmission of international disturbances, (prior to the 1970s, and going back as far as the nineteenth century, developing countries had always had relatively little or no floating-interest debt). Indeed, it has been argued[6] that variable-interest loans imply that one of the central functions of a financial system—the effective transfer of risk—was not efficiently served, as the risks were passed exclusively to borrowers rather than shared with the banks or depositors. Price instability, long a

Table 8.1. Some current account indicators, Latin America
(US $ billion)

	1975	1980	1981	1982	1983
a. Net payments of profits and interests	5.7	18.5	28.0	37.0	33.9
b. Balance on current account	−13.7	−27.7	−40.4	−36.4	−8.5

Source : ECLAC, *Adjustment Policies and the Renegotiation of External Debt*, 20th session, Lima, Peru, 29 March–6 April 1984, E/CEPAL/6.1299, E/CEPAL/SES.20/6.17.

feature of commodity trade, had become also a feature of the transfer of financial resources; this created an additional source of uncertainty for developing countries' balance of payments, relating to the level of future servicing of already contracted debt. It implied in particular that the stance and mix of fiscal and monetary policy in industrial countries (and especially in the USA) would have strong impact on developing countries, via its influence on interest rates in the international banking sector.

In the early 1980s, the trends *both* in commodity prices *and* in interest rates were simultaneously unfavourable for developing countries, with a disastrous impact on their current account deficits.

3. A third factor which magnified the impact of the recession on all developing countries, but particularly so for the Latin American ones, was the large decline in bank lending to them, precisely because bankers' perceptions of credit risk in such lending was sharply increased by the rapid deterioration in those countries' current account balances. The growing inability of so many of the major debtor countries to service their debts since 1982, and the obvious need to reschedule such debts (with the threat of a possible default lurking in the background) discouraged new bank loans to those—and other—Latin American countries. Thus, the debt crises were in some cases made worse—or even precipitated—by the self-fulfilling fears of private bankers and their unwillingness to lend to particular countries. These trends would doubtless have become much more marked had not the

IMF, BIS, and industrial countries' central banks stepped in, as described below.

The pro-cyclical nature of private international lending is not a new phenomenon, but seems to be almost a structural feature of such lending. Kindleberger, for example,[7] has described how the present pro-cyclical link of bank lending with the business cycle (both in periods of growth and decline) has many historical precedents, going back as far as the eighteenth century.

The impact on Latin American economies of the sharp decline in international bank lending was particularly serious. On the one hand, the decline occurred after a rather long period during which the net inflow of loans had risen considerably, and during which not only the external sector but also the *overall operation* of most Latin American economies had become increasingly dependent and reliant upon this constant increase of external finance (based on a more or less explicit but incorrect assumption that such levels would continue). On the other hand, the decline in net inflow of capital coincided not only with a sharp fall in commodity prices, but also with the increased cost of servicing previously contracted variable-interest debt (which, as pointed out, was an additional element of instability and uncertainty of the international financial system). As a result, there was a dramatic reversal in the direction of the transfer of resources between Latin America and the rest of the world. This phenomenon and its implications have not yet been fully perceived, either in the Latin American continent or abroad.

As shown in Table 8.2, betwen 1981 and 1983 net capital inflows to Latin America are estimated to have fallen by US $33.3 billion, while net payments of profit and interest grew by US $6.8 billion; as a result, net transfer of resources declined by US $40 billion in those two years to a level of −US $30 billion in 1983. While during 1981 the positive net transfer of resources added almost 9 per cent to Latin America's importing capacity (in the late 1970s it had added much more), in 1983 the negative net transfer subtracted from Latin America's importing capacity the equivalent of around 30 per cent of its exports of goods and services. It can therefore be concluded that, particularly during the early 1980s, the negative impact of the sharp reversal of net transfers of resources (equivalent to almost 40 per cent of the region's exports between 1981 and 1983) was far more serious than the impact of the

Table 8.2. Latin America: net transfer of resources, 1970–84

	Net capital inflow US $ bn. (1)	Net payment of profits and interest US $ bn. (2)	Net transfer of resources US $ bn. $(3)=(1)-(2)$	(3) as proportion of exports of goods and services (4)
1970	4.2	3.0	1.2	6.7
1973	7.8	4.2	3.6	12.5
1976	18.2	6.8	11.4	24.1
1978	26.1	10.2	15.9	25.9
1979	28.6	13.6	15.0	18.3
1980	30.0	18.0	12.0	11.3
1981	37.7	27.7	10.0	8.8
1982	19.2	37.6	-18.4	-18.1
1983	4.4	34.5	-30.0	-30.0
1984	10.6	37.3	-26.7	-23.6

Source: ECLAC, *Preliminary Overview of the Latin American Economy during 1984*, Santiago de Chile, January 1985.

deterioration of trade during those years (which ECLAC estimates at around 14 per cent).

Furthermore, for three years already (1982–4), Latin America has continuously been a net exporter of financial resources, and the prospects that this will change in the near future are not good. We will discuss below both the economic and the political implications of the abnormal situation whereby developing countries are net exporters of financial resources.

4. A fourth factor that magnified the impact of the industrial countries' recession on Latin America, often ignored in existing analysis, was the rise in the dollar exchange rate, which increased the effective cost to most countries of the interest and amortization payments on their external debt.

The lack of a new agent for international financial intermediation

From the point of view of our previous analysis, in the initial chapters, one of the most important characteristics of Latin America's external finance in the early 1980s is that, unlike the previous three decades, *there has not emerged a new dynamic actor* who perceived rapidly increasing flows towards the region as the policy most advantageous to his perceived interests. At the same time, the actors (both public and private) who played such a role in past decades now seem unwilling to do so to the same extent. There is therefore a serious danger that, for the rest of the decade, the process of international financial intermediation from industrial countries to Latin American countries will be on a scale greatly reduced from that in the second half of the 1970s; as a result, in the short term growth will continue to suffer in the region while, in the medium term, *only* strategies with far less dependence on foreign financial flows will be viable. The debate whether private or official lenders should play a leading role is clearly interesting, but remains irrelevant while neither type of agent is willing or able to play such a role!

A further weakness of the system of international financial intermediation, and one that has become far more evident during the last world recession, is the inadequacy of existing counter-cyclical or compensatory financial mechanisms.

Instability in national economies has led to generally increased recognition of the role of automatic stabilizing devices within national economies over the past few decades. There has been little parallel growth in automatic stabilizing mechanisms at the international level, even though the need to increase international action to provide defences and moderate the impact of recessions is perceived as essential by economists belonging to different schools of thought.

Amongst the most important elements in automatic or quasi-automatic stabilization at the international level are those relating to the provision of stable and adequate official liquidity. One such mechanism is the issue of SDRs to 'supplement existing reserve assets in such a manner as will avoid economic stagnation and deflation as well as excess demand·inflation in the world' (as the IMF established in Article 18 of its Agreements). There is, however, no concrete or automatic criterion to decide on new issues of SDRs, and in spite of quite wide professional consensus about the need for new SDR allocations in recent years, no such issue has been carried out since 1981.

Another potentially important mechanism for enhancing international liquidity is the provision of low-conditionality lending by the IMF (which is the only part of its lending that can be appropriately included in international liquidity). However, the capacity of the IMF to provide such resources has been significantly curtailed by the fact that IMF quotas (which determine the amount of resources available to the Fund, and each member's relative access to those resources) have been allowed to lag well behind the growth of international trade—declining from 16 per cent of world trade when the Fund was created in 1944 to 4 per cent at the start of the 1980s, and even lagging further behind the evolution of the magnitude of current account imbalances. As a result, the IMF lacked both the resources and a clear mandate from member countries to foster smooth adjustment via semi-automatic mechanisms.

The limited counter-cyclical facilities that do exist were created largely as result of pressure from developing countries. In fact, the creation of the IMF's Compensatory Financing Facility (CFF) in 1963 was the first change in the rules of the international monetary system that developing countries suceeded in securing.[8] The CFF's stated objective is to maintain unaffected import capacity, in the face of export fluctuations caused by external events, through the provision of relatively low-conditionality credit.

Different studies have shown that borrowing under the CFF remained relatively modest, particularly in relation to the magnitude of the terms-of-trade deterioration experienced in the early 1980s by developing countries.[9] The main problem with the existing *modus operandi* of the CFF was identified as the limit on maximum drawing.[10]

Different liberalizations of the CFF have been suggested so as to provide full (or at least larger than existing at the time) coverage of export shortfalls, either by eliminating the link between the size of the drawing allowed as a percentage of the country's quota, or by increasing the limit. Linked to the emergence of widespread debt crises in the early 1980s, there arose in many circles[11] the proposal that the *IMF's compensatory financing facility should also provide loans to offset fluctuations in interest rates*. This modification would have had the merit of reducing the impact of one of the key new sources of international economic instability (large fluctuations in interest rates) by adapting a mechanism which already deals with the more traditional sources of instability, related to export earnings. A CFF thus modified (or another mechanism on similar lines) would have attempted to stabilize countries' import capacity (and compensate for externally caused fluctuations in export prices, import prices, and interest rates) in cases of balance of payments need. Powerful counter-cyclical instruments, such as an expanded CFF, would make a major contribution not only to reducing the impact of shocks in the international economy on individual developing countries, but also to reducing instability in the world economy as a whole. Given that, as we have seen, one of the main features of the world economy since the early 1970s has been increased instability in key variables, and that this instability and the resultant uncertainty is seen as negative by different types of economic agents, and by different schools of economic thought, measures to enhance prospects for future stability could be expected to have a broader base of support than the potentially more controversial issue of systematically increasing financial flows to LDC's, as the 'mutuality' of interests seems far clearer in the former.

In this context, it seems particularly problematic that suggestions of the type outlined above have not been followed up; on the contrary, in fact, the limits on drawings under the CFF, as a proportion of countries' quotas, have been reduced, albeit in relation to enhanced quotas. Of greater concern is the fact that, in September 1983, the IMF Executive Board[12] passed a resolution which significantly alters the conditions under which the CFF drawings can be made. Up until September 1983, the first half of CFF drawings required only *willingness* on the part of the country 'to co-operate with the Fund in an effort to find, where required, appropriate solutions for its balance of payments difficulties', which implied that the drawing had in practice had very little conditionality attached to it, and that it could therefore be granted semi-automatically and speedily. The modified resolution says now that readiness to co-operate 'implies a willingness to receive Fund missions and to discuss, in good faith, the appropriateness of the member's policies and whether changes in the member's policies are necessary to deal with its balance of payments difficulties'. The fact that a country has established that it has experienced a temporary export shortfall (as defined by the Fund) for reasons beyond its control no longer provides sufficient ground for a CFF drawing. As a result of these changes, the main existing international counter-cyclical facility to fund temporary problems (outside the particular government's control) has been severely weakened by being linked to a level of conditionality that may be either undesirable or unacceptable for that government. Adjustment, without even significant temporary counter-cyclical, low-conditionality funding, is what the international financial system demands from developing countries with balance of payments problems, independently of the causes of such problems!

'National' causes of Latin American crises

Even though the deterioration in the international environment clearly precipitated in the early 1980s the widespread crises both of debt and of development, the strategies and economic policies pursued at the time—and previously—by Latin American governments (as well as the actions of Latin American private agents) were a major contributory factor to the depth of those crises.

The severity with which the deterioration in the international environment affected different economies was obviously linked to the use made by those economies of the large increase in their foreign debt that occurred during the 1970s, and to the impact which foreign flows had (or were allowed to have) on macroeconomic policies. This was linked at a broader level to the degree to which different Latin American economies and societies had responded to the abundance of foreign flows by opening up and de-regulating their financial and trade systems. The relative abundance of foreign exchange, the degree of opening up of the economy, and the macroeconomic policies pursued determined in individual countries the extent to which a transnationalized segment of the national economy was consolidated, which was characterized in all cases by life-styles and consumption patterns with a very high and dynamic import content; abundance of foreign exchange, as well as open and de-regulated financial flows, also made capital flight feasible on a far larger scale than had occurred in the past.

It seems useful in this context, to distinguish the purposes for which increases in the foreign debt can be used.[13] Increases in foreign debt can correspond to short-term compensatory borrowing in response to cyclical declines in the purchasing power of exports, to longer-term borrowing to smooth structural adjustment to external or domestic shocks, to borrowing to increase imported national consumption or imports of arms, and to borrowing which ultimately funds capital flight.

Increasing evidence has emerged that, particularly in the case of some Latin American economies, a very high proportion of foreign inflows in the late 1970s and early 1980s were devoted either to capital flight or to increased imports of non-essential consumption goods. To take an extreme example, the case of Argentina, several analysts[14] have concluded that, during the 1974–82 period, practically all the increase in the foreign debt was being used, not for funding trade deficits, but *de facto* for private capital outflows, private acquisition of foreign assets, or net service payments on previously accumulated foreign debt. Less widely discussed are the estimates of the US Federal Reserve System Board of Governors, which also reflect a similar outcome for Venezuela, a country which had large trade surpluses for the 1974–82 period, but whose foreign debt significantly increased during those years, mainly reflecting capital flight and servicing of previously accumulated debt. An important, though somewhat smaller, proportion of the increase in the Mexican foreign debt is reported to have funded capital flight and service payments during those years.

It is interesting to stress here that the countries which seem to have experienced very little capital flight during that period (that is, Colombia and Brazil amongst the major Latin American countries, and Asian economies such as South Korea or Thailand) were all characterized both by fairly stringent capital controls and by avoidance of gross overvaluation of exchange controls.[15] Though difficult to control (given the abundance of international private lending during the 1970s and the tendency for private 'transnationalized' individuals to escape with their wealth abroad, attracted by secure and high yields abroad compared with risky and unstable conditions nationally), capital flight was thus not an inevitable evil; capital flight could be significantly reduced by governments which were prudent both in the extent to which they opened their economies to foreign inflows and outflows and in their management of the relevant macroeconomic variables.

There was a second level in which the 'transnationalization' or opening up of Latin American economies led to inappropriate use of foreign debt increases. The case that illustrates this trend to the extreme is that of Chile, where a combination of very rapid dismantling of trade barriers and overvaluation of the exchange rate—led to a dramatic increase in the import of non-food consumption goods, a large proportion of which were luxury or non-essential goods consumed mainly by the upper-income strata. Between 1970 and 1981, the value of these non-food consumption imports grew by 1.093 per cent, while total imports during that period grew by 127 per cent, and fuel imports increased by 484 per cent. Perfumes and cosmetic imports are estimated to have increased by 19.500 per cent; television sets imports by 9.357 per cent, and alcoholic drinks and tobacco by 2.400 per cent; the import of cars and motorcycles grew in value by 1.248 per cent during the period.[16] The import of automobiles was immense not only in percentage terms but also as a proportion of the existing stock; it thus created an important increase in future demand for oil, spare parts, etc., a very high proportion of which are necessarily imported. This illustrated how the problem was not just the increase in imports during particular years, but the increased future dependence of the Chilean economy on a higher level of imported inputs. This spectacular growth in Chilean imports of non-essential consumer goods meant that, by 1981, over 20 per cent of total Chilean imports were made up of 'non-traditional' luxury items (whereas in 1970 this percentage had been negligible); furthermore, in 1981, the volume of these imports was equivalent to half the very large trade deficit in that year!

A high proportion, therefore, of the increase in the Chilean foreign debt since 1974 was channelled towards increased imports of consumption goods, many of them of a 'superfluous' nature. Furthermore, the period of increased borrowing since 1974 coincided with a *decline* in the rate of investment as a proportion of GDP; the capacity of the economy to service the foreign debt in the future was reduced, while the magnitude óf the foreign debt was rapidly increased.

As imports were competing on increasingly favourable terms with domestic industry (due to both tariff reductions and exchange rate appreciations), it can be argued that, in Chile, the increase in the foreign debt sustained (or made easier) a process which *de facto* led to de-industrialization; this was reflected in the systematic decline in the real value of industrial output between 1972 and 1982.[17]

In the case of countries like Argentina and Chile, large capital inflows contributed to a debt-led deficit in the balance of payments, and to the creation of unsustainable distortions in the national economies. Use of foreign debt was clearly different in a number of countries, such as Brazil or South Korea, that used the increased level of foreign savings during the 1970s to support high investment ratios (which increased significantly as a proportion of GNP during the 1970s), and to sustain growth in the face of severe deterioration in these countries' terms of trade.

More broadly, a review of these and other cases in the 1970s[18] seems to suggest that the increase in the foreign debt made on the whole a somewhat more positive contribution to growth and development if (*a*) flows of capital (both into and out of the country) were regulated, (*b*) foreign inflows entered an economy where the state had a clear 'vision' of a development strategy, and where—directly or indirectly—it played an important role in investment, and (*c*) where deliberate policies were pursued by the state to orientate market forces (for example in international trade and in international capital markets) towards sustained growth in specific productive sectors.

However, vulnerability of growth to a severe deterioration in the international economic environment was not only a feature of 'open and de-regulated economies', such as those of Chile and Argentina, but also affected seriously—though to a lesser degree— countries such as Brazil, whose governments had attempted a more pragmatic and gradual 'opening up' of their economies to trade, and where the state had attempted to define a coherent development strategy, but which had nevertheless relied heavily on substantial net foreign finance and expanding foreign markets to sustain such growth.

Recent reductions and instability of net external financial flows, the conditionality attached to an increasing proportion of these flows, and the unstable growth of world trade in the early 1980s, would seem to make it more attractive to developing countries' governments to rely in the future relatively less on development strategies that are export-led and debt-sustained, and emphasize— to the extent that it is feasible—production for the internal market and reliance on national savings. We will return to this theme in the last chapter.

The 'management' of the Latin American debt crises

For Latin American countries, the wave of debt crises and reschedulings began in August 1982, when the Mexican government declared a moratorium on repayments of capital on the public sector debt. Although debt crises had previously occurred in a few Latin American (and other developing, particularly African) countries, only relatively small debts had been involved. Mexico's debt crisis was perceived differently, given that Mexico was the second largest debtor to the banks in the third world.

Mexico's debt-servicing difficulties—followed by the emergence of similar problems in other large Latin American debtor countries—caused serious concern amongst the international banks, as they feared that such difficulties (and the danger of their leading to outright default) could threaten their profitability and even their existence.

The banks' reaction was to restrict credit quickly, not just to the countries already experiencing debt crises, but to practically all the other Latin American countries. This led to a very sharp decline in new bank lending to Latin America. During the year and a half before mid-1982, total new lending to Latin America reached US $42 billion; in the year and a half after mid-1982, new lending to Latin America fell to less than one-fourth of that amount, to US $9 billion.[19] This contraction of credit made debt servicing even more difficult for the rest of the borrowers. By the beginning of 1985, the only important Latin American country to avoid debt rescheduling was Colombia.

Although debt crises became so widespread, and although their management had a 'cliff-hanging' character to it, the operation was successful in avoiding a major default or any other action that could have potentially precipitated a major international banking crisis, even though the banks' own 'creditworthiness' diminished somewhat. On the other hand, Latin American countries were far more seriously hurt by the debt crises than were the banks, as the former were forced to contract their economies so as to be able to continue servicing their debt.

The details of debt crisis management have been described elsewhere.[20] Here we shall concentrate only on what seem to be the main structural features of this process.

1. A first feature of the debt crisis management in the 1980s was

that industrial countries' central banks and governments, as well as official international organizations, came back to the centre of the stage (almost abandoned to private actors during the previous ten years).

Of particular importance was the IMF's key role in assembling 'rescue packages' which have simultaneously included an upper credit tranche (high-conditionality) programme with the Fund, rescheduling of maturing debts, and arrangement of new finance from banks. The BIS and the US Treasury have also played an important role in several cases; this has included the granting of crucial 'bridging' loans while the 'package deals' were being assembled.

2. The new finance from private banks has to a large extent been granted on an 'involuntary' basis. In several cases (particularly, but not only, in the case of major debtors), the IMF and the industrial countries' central banks have told the private banks by exactly what percentage they 'must', collectively and individually, increase their lending; the IMF has itself refused to agree to lend to a particular country until private banks committed themselves to make new loans for a certain sum of money.

The Fund's influence became crucial as, for the first time, adjustment financing provided by the IMF was conditional not only upon policy changes in the debtor country, but also upon the extension of new credit by private international banks.

Analytically, this has an important implication. Since 1982, the IMF has to a significant extent 'created' a market, by encouraging or even pressing private banks to lend where they did not necessarily wish to do so. The BIS in its recent Annual Report talks about a 'split market, with no new spontaneous lending to Latin America in 1983 and 1984'. We would like to go beyond this and argue that a 'non-spontaneous market' is in fact not a market in the sense conventionally accepted by economic theory, and that *de facto*, in the period after mid-1982, a proper market of lending to Latin America largely ceased to exist, as practically all lending that occurred was non-spontaneous, and was associated with conditional credits from the IMF. (Indeed, during 1984, total new bank lending to non-OPEC Latin America was significantly *lower* than the total level obtained by these countries from the banks under IMF-sponsored credit packages, which implies that there were offsetting *reductions* of other bank credits.)

Banks heavily involved in LDC lending welcomed, or possibly even encouraged, the IMF's move to organize rescheduling of private debt and of new lending, as they perceived correctly that this diminished the risk of open default by particular countries. Smaller banks often seem to have resented this new role assumed by the IMF. For example, S. M. Yassukovich, managing director of a small Euro-market bank, told the *Financial Times* conference on 15 December 1982:

For the first time in our history as independent bankers we have been robbed of our freedom of action in taking a decision on whether to make a loan or not. We have been told that if we don't make a loan, our standing in the market could be prejudiced. It seems to be a fundamental interference with the independence of bankers. If people think through the implications of that they will be horrified. It is going to accelerate the process of people dropping out of the market.

The last point is a very crucial one. Private banks (particularly, but to an increasing degree not only, the smaller banks), perceive it as undesirable that when their loans run into difficulty, they have not only to renegotiate them but also to lend more to those countries, following the dictates of the IMF and their central banks; as a result, they are therefore increasingly withdrawing (either permanently or temporarily) from the syndicated and short-term loan market.

3. A third feature of debt crisis management has been the formation of steering committees by the private banks, for the purpose of negotiating with the debtor governments. It is these steering committees—a sort of cartel of banks—which have conducted negotiations on rescheduling and new loans, reached tentative agreements with governments on this subject, and then—often with the support of their own central banks as well as that of the IMF—pressed smaller or other banks with debt outstanding from that country to accept the 'package deal'. Particularly problematic has been the agreement by smaller banks to increase their exposure by a certain percentage (as the IMF and the big banks wished) which in fact represented a partial capitalization of interest.

4. Negotiations have been conducted, as regards the debtors, on a case-by-case basis. This implies that while both the private creditors (through the steering committee) and the official

international creditor institutions (such as the IMF and the BIS) act in a co-ordinated manner, they are able to deal with each individual debtor country on a separate basis. Although during 1984 most of the Latin American debtor governments have successfully 'politicized' the debt problem by meetings and joint statements on the subject, their actions have not broken the pattern of negotiations whereby creditors negotiate as a bloc while debtors negotiate individually.

Even though the meetings and declarations of the so-called Cartagena group of Latin American debtors have not succeeded in achieving a major change in the process and outcome of negotiations, there is evidence that the activities of this group have somewhat strengthened the position of the debtors. As a very knowledgeable but fairly orthodox observer, William Cline[21] has recognized:

The overall effect of these developments [in mid-1984] was a distinct shift in the negotiating climate towards greater politicization and, conceivably, aggressiveness on the part of the major debtors, and towards greater accommodation (but always within the framework of a market-related solution rather than debt forgiveness) on the part of banks, Western governments and the IMF.

5. A further characteristic of recent lending and rescheduling is the difficulty and complexity of these operations. Not only do official international institutions (such as the IMF and BIS) have to co-ordinate among themselves and negotiate often hotly debated agreements with the government of the debtor country; all these economic actors have to reach agreement with a large number of creditor commercial banks (which, in the case of Mexico, was reported in 1983 to reach 1,400)! As a result, much time is spent by senior representatives of Latin American governments in these negotiations; much of the private bankers' and IMF officials' time and energy is also spent in these matters. The complexity of the task, and the difficulties in reaching agreement, have in a number of cases implied that agreement is delayed beyond the targeted time, and the situation has been further complicated by the need for special bridging loans. The banks initially not only charged for the time spent on these operations but also made an additional profit on them, particularly during the first two years of debt crisis management (for example, in high penalty margins and refinancing

fees). This practice was not only absurd, increasing the long-term debt service for countries already unable to meet the existing burden, but was in sharp contrast with many domestic restructuring arrangements made by the same banks in their own countries, which provide for somewhat reduced lending rates to help a borrower back on his feet. As a result of pressures from the debtor countries, in the course of 1984, such additional costs have been reduced or eliminated.

6. The complexity of the negotiations was accentuated by the fact that debt rescheduling (of both private and official debt) followed the 'short-leash', year-by-year approach. This approach imposed by the creditors implied the consolidation of debt corresponding to only one year of payments, which has in some cases led to an almost continuous process of negotiation. The uncertainty associated with the availability of financing, its terms, and the nature of the guarantees cover an important part of the negotation period, causing disruptions to the normal economic operations of the country, and introduce additional uncertainty in already unsettled international financial markets. This problem is well illustrated by the case of the Paris Club reschedulings of official debt, as export credit cover is often interrupted while the country is preparing for a Paris Club meeting, and while it has not signed the individual bilateral agreements with each creditor.

Multi-year rescheduling, at least of debt to banks (as first ratified between Mexico and its creditors in early 1985), was therefore an important procedural step towards reducing the pressure on negotiators both for debtors and for creditors. It is unfortunate that multi-year rescheduling had not by early 1985 been accepted as a general norm, but was granted mainly for larger debtors and/or those who were seen by creditors to have 'behaved well' in their previous adjustment efforts. It should be stressed here that, although multi-year rescheduling has very important procedural advantages (for both creditors and, particularly, debtors), it has not implied that the net transfer of resources from the country to the private creditors changes significantly, even less that it becomes positive.

7. The complexity of the negotiations related to debt crisis management, combined with the need to repeat these operations on a yearly basis, have meant that senior government and IMF officials, as well as bankers, spend a very high proportion of their

time in travelling, and in meetings to arrange or patch up agreements. Although costly and inefficient also to them, this focus on debt crisis management has been broadly functional with respect to the main target of private bankers—pursuing the stability of the banking system. From the point of view of the developing countries, the priority on negotiations imposed by the 'needs' of debt crisis management, as defined fundamentally by the banks and the IMF, has distracted attention and energy from what should be the main concern of developing countries' governments, that is, their countries' growth and development. It probably is not unfair to say that most Latin American governments have since 1982 devoted more time and priority to ensuring that the Fund's performance criteria are met, and that the rescheduling packages are assembled, than to the design of viable medium-term development strategies.

Evaluation of debt rescheduling

At a deeper level, the results of the 'package deals'—as regards rescheduling, new flows, and, in almost every case, a high-conditionality agreement with the Fund (although such deals provide some important short-term breathing space from foreign exchange constraints by significant reductions in debt service ratio)—have, in the case of the Latin American countries, entailed a very significant negative transfer of financial resources since 1982. As a result, the focus of economic policy has been on the need to generate a sufficiently large trade surplus (whatever the cost to the domestic economy) to allow the funding of this negative net transfer of resources.

In the past, many Latin American countries have often accepted IMF conditionality as a prerequisite for obtaining net financial resources from abroad, when they perceived that the additional flows obtained thanks to the Fund's 'seal of approval' outweighed the cost of loss of autonomy in policy-making that agreements with the Fund implied. Since 1982, Latin American countries have been accepting IMF conditionality which is at least as problematic as in previous periods, but without even the beneficial counterpart that agreements with the Fund will encourage a net inflow of resources from abroad, as, on the contrary, practically all the 'package deals' imply a net outflow of financial resources. It seems that, were such a situation to continue, its absurdity would eventually make it politically unacceptable to a variety of Latin American governments.

It is indeed surprising that Latin American governments and policy-makers have basically accepted as inevitable this form of 'debt crisis management'. Although they have objected to specific aspects of the rescheduling deals (for example, refinancing fees and excessive stringency of IMF performance criteria) and have obtained some fairly minor concessions, governments—particularly collectively—have not challenged their willingness and ability to continue indefinitely making net transfers of financial resources.

It would seem that Latin American governments have not fully perceived their new bargaining strength. When the net financial flows are positive to a developing country, then the greater bargaining strength lies with the lender, as it is he who must ultimately decide to make the new loan and transfer the funds; as a result, the lender can easily impose all types of conditions, particularly to governments desperately in need of foreign exchange. When there are negative financial flows from a debtor developing country, the greater bargaining strength has potentially shifted to the debtor government, as it is the party which must decide to repay and ultimately to make the transfers of funds; as a result, the debtor is in this case in the strong position, not only to resist the conditions of the lender but, even more fundamentally, to impose its own. Thus, the Latin American governments not only could have resisted far more strongly the conditions imposed by their creditors (such as increased cost of rescheduling and stringency of IMF adjustment programmes) but could also have demanded their own terms as a pre-condition for their transfer of large financial resources to the creditors.

We believe that the type of reforms which such debtors could have demanded, and should in future demand as a condition of effecting net transfers from their economies relate to a more adequate system of international financial intermediation, which would generate more stable and predictable flows to developing countries (for example, by regular issues of SDR's, broadening of semi-automatic compensatory facilities, and guarantees for private flows). Interestingly, it may also be argued that many of those changes, if introduced, would be clearly to the benefit not only of the debtor countries' economies but of the whole international economy. At present, the conventional wisdom in international financial circles is to evaluate whether LDC governments will disrupt the international financial system; perhaps the key question to ask is, on the contrary, whether they can exert enough effective pressure to make it far stronger and more efficient.

To be able to play such a constructive role, Latin American governments would have to take a far broader view than they have done hitherto. As Dornbusch[22] has pointed out, Latin American governments have

accepted to make external debt a narrow technical problem (with vast domestic costs) rather than a burning international issue. They have come to accept (wrongly) that solving the debt problem is solely an issue of economics: forecasts of interest rates, growth rates, etc are at the center of the discussion to determine what are the domestic policies consistent with a dramatic reduction in their external indebtedness.

Yet, as Dornbusch clearly states, and as some Latin American leaders are beginning to perceive, 'solving debt problems is mostly politics, not economics'. We will pursue this crucial theme further in the next chapter, where we will try to outline ways forward that would be both technically and politically acceptable.

Notes

1. J. Sachs, 'Comments' on C. Diaz-Alejandro, 'Latin American Debt: I Don't Think We Are in Kansas Anymore', *Brookings Papers on Economic Activity* 2, 1984.
2. Diaz-Alejandro, 'Latin American Debt'.
3. UNCTAD, *Trade and Development Report 1984*, New York, July 1984.
4. ECLAC, *Preliminary Overview of the Latin American Economy During 1984*, Santiago de Chile, January 1985.
5. See UNCTAD, *Trade and Development Report 1984* for more details.
6. D. Llewellyn 'The International Monetary System since 1972, Structural Change and Financial Innovation', paper presented to IMF/ODI Seminar, 'International Monetary Adaptation', March 1985.
7. C. Kindleberger, *Manias, Panics and Crashes*, London, 1978.
8. There are also two smaller compensatory financing schemes in existence, which are not however of relevance to Latin America (one

is administered by the Arab Monetary fund, while the other, STABEX, is administered by the European Community).
9. See, for example, J. Williamson 'The Lending Policies of the IMF', in J. Williamson, ed., *IMF Conditionality*, Cambridge, Mass., 1983.
10. See, for example, S. Griffith-Jones 'Compensatory Financing Facility: A Review of its Opeation and Proposals for Improvement', Report to the Group of 24, UNDP/UNCTAD Project INT/81/046, June 1983.
11. See Chapter 10 for details.
12. See IMF Executive Board Resolution, 'Compensatory Financing of Export Fluctuations: Guidelines on Cooperation' (83/140), in IMF, *Annual Report 1984*, Washington, DC; and S. Dell, 'The Fifth Credit Tranche' (mimeo, New York, 1984), for a criticism of this resolution.
13. See also R. Ffrench Davies, 'International Private Lending and Borrowing Strategies of Developing Countries', *Journal of Development Planning* 14, 1984, where a similar classification is developed.
14. See, for example, J. Schvarzer, 'The Foreign Debt: An Unorthodox Approach from the Debtor's Point of View', in *Debt Crisis in Latin America*, Institute of Latin American Studies Monograph 13, Stockholm, 1986; R. Dornbusch, *External Debt, Budget Deficits and Disequilibrium Exchange Rates*, Massachusetts, Institute of Technology Working Paper 347, June 1984; Federal Reserve System Board of Governors, International Finance Discussion Paper 227, 'An Analysis of External Debt Positions of Eight Developing Countries through 1990'; C. Diaz-Alejandro, 'Latin American Debt: I Don't Think We Are in Kansas Anymore'; and, for a detailed study, B. Lischinsky *The Argentinian Foreign Debt, its Internal Economic Impact, 1955–81*, M. Phil. thesis, Institute of Social Studies, The Hague, May 1985.
15. Diaz-Alejandro, 'I Don't Think We Are in Kansas Anymore'.
16. For detailed figures, see R. Ffrench-Davies. *El Experimento Monetarista en Chile: Una Sintesis Critica*, Coleccion Estudios CIEPLAN 9, Santiago de Chile, December 1982; and *Liberalizacion de las Importaciones, la Experiencia Chilena, 1973–79*, Coleccion Estudios CIEPLAN 4, Santiago de Chile, November 1980.
17. For more details see, for example, S. Griffith-Jones and E. Rodriquez, 'Private International Finance and Industrialization of LDCs', *Journal of Development Studies* 21(1), October 1984.
18. See, for example, S. Dell and R. Lawrence, *The Balance of Payments Adjustment Process in Developing Countries*, New York, 1980; and S. Griffith-Jones and C. Harvey (eds.), *World Prices and Development*, Aldershot, 1985.
19. BIS, *International Banking Developments*, Basle, April 1984.
20. See the international financial press for blow-by-blow accounts; for a more synthetic treatment, see for example ECLAC, *Adjustment*

Policies and Renegotiation of the External Debt, 20th session, Lima, Peru, 29 March–6 April 1984, E /CEPAL /6.1299,E /CEPAL /SES.20 / 6.17. and IMF Occasional Paper 31, *Recent Multilateral Debt Restructurings with Official and Bank Creditors*, Washington, DC, December 1983.
21. W. Cline, *International Debt: Systemic Risk and Policy Response*, Cambridge, Mass., 1984, Ch. 8.
22. R. Dornbusch, 'The Debt Problem: 1980–84 and Beyond', mimeo, Massachusetts Institute of Technology, Cambridge, Mass., January 1985.

CHAPTER 9

Will the Industrial Countries' Recovery 'solve' the Crises of Debt and National Development in Latin America?

In the next chapter we will explore in more depth the types of options for change in the international financial system which Latin American governments could press for, given their enhanced bargaining power.

Before doing so, we will first further examine whether recovery in industrial countries, allied to the current strategy of debt crisis management with marginal improvements, is likely to be sufficient at the same time to 'solve' or 'overcome' the crises of debt and national development in Latin America.

This was indeed the view widely held, particularly towards the middle and end of 1984, by industrial countries' governments, international financial institutions and multinational banks. Though continuing to be the 'official line' in early 1985, confidence in a complacent analysis was being challenged, for example, by problems with the 'package deals' between Brazil and Argentina and their creditors,[1] and by the rapid slow-down of the US economy.

The optimistic—or complacent—line was clearly articulated by the IMF, in its 1984 *World Economic Outlook*:

Assuming moderate rates of growth in the industrial countries, some fall in real interest rates, and unchanged terms of trade, and assuming also that the non-oil developing countries continue their present adjustment policies, the conclusions is reached that most groups of those countries can achieve adequate rates of growth of GDP (although somewhat below the rates attained during the 1960's and 1970's), while restoring a manageable position with respect to their current accounts and debt-service ratios.[2]

Although with more reservations than the IMF, William Cline[3] states, as a basic conclusion to his 1984 study: 'the problem of international debt is likely to recede as international economic recovery proceeds—and it remains appropriate to manage the problem as one of illiquidity, not insolvency, and on a case-by-case basis'.

There are several very major problems with these optimistic views. First, there are doubts about the plausibility of the scenarios projected, because there are a number of pre-conditions whose realism is individually dubious, and which would need to be satisfied *simultaneously*, just to make debt service viable. Secondly, and far more importantly, even the most optimistic scenarios assume very low growth for Latin America countries for the rest of the decade, implying that, by 1990, living standards (particularly of the working class) would at best be equal to, if not below, their 1980 levels. Thirdly, it is assumed that debtor countries will agree to continue reducing their debts (relative to exports) by trade surpluses—preferably by growth of exports but, if this proves not to be possible, by reduction of imports; until this objective is achieved, austerity and adjustment would continue to be required from Latin American countries. The rather doubtful prize offered for such a policy is the restoration of 'creditworthiness' in the distant future, and the resumption then by banks of 'voluntary lending'; there is, however, no assurance that this will occur in the near future, and, if anything, the evidence from recent trends, and from numerous declarations by bankers and central bankers in industrial countries, is that it is rather unlikely.[4] Few practitioners would dispute, in 1985, Fishlow's[5] conclusion: 'According to all present signs and past historical reaction to external debt problems, *voluntary lending will not recuperate quickly*'. A Commonwealth Secretariat Report issued in April 1985 similarly concluded: 'Even if debtor countries are able to restore market perceptions of creditworthiness, bank regulators and bank shareholders will act as strong restraining influences on developing countries exposure.'

There is also an implicit assumption in the more sophisticated optimistic analysis that, once sufficient adjustment has been carried out and the 'debt crisis is over', other forms of private finance, more appropriate for development finance than variable-interest banking credit, will play an important role in providing net funding.[6] However, even the more optimistic projections, such as those of Lessard and Williamson, estimated rather marginal increases in such flows (for example, direct investment, quasi-equity, bonds) until the end of the decade, unless major changes were to be made in the role played by public institutions in international financial intermediation.

While the costs of adjustment for Latin American countries are real and immediate, the potential benefits of such adjustment are hypothetical, small, and likely to materialize only in the rather distant future!

In what follows, we will review briefly the evidence from the recent past, as well as discussing future projections to show that it seems highly unlikely that this circle can be squared, and that—without fundamental changes in the *modus operandi* of the international financial system, as well as of national development strategies—the crises of debt and of development in Latin America cannot simultaneously be overcome.

The impact of industrial countries' recovery

It is clear that the vigorous US recovery in 1983, and particularly in 1984 (US real GNP is estimated by the OECD[7] to have grown by 3.7 per cent in 1983 and by 6.75 per cent in 1984, accompanied by a much slower recovery in the rest of the industrial countries), has had important beneficial effects both on moderating the seriousness of the debt crises and on contributing to the restoration of very modest growth in Latin America during 1984.

As discussed in Chapter 2, Latin America's GDP is estimated to have grown in 1984 by 2.6 per cent; GDP per capita, however, grew by a mere 0.2 per cent. Although this was an improvement over the 1982–3 period, when GDP fell, Latin America's 1984 growth was clearly meagre in per capita terms, and well below average historical trends. Furthermore, Latin American GDP per capita was in 1984 still 9 per cent lower than in 1980, and reached only the level that the region had already attained in 1976!

The recovery of the Latin American economies in 1984 was so slight that it would not have been able even to begin to restore to previous levels crucial items for current welfare, such as social expenditure, and for future growth and employment, such as fixed capital formation. It is noteworthy that the level of fixed capital formation between 1981 and 1983 is estimated by ECLAC to have declined by approximately 40 per cent. Such a decline—unless rapidly reversed—will imply a serious constraint on future expansion of production, either for the internal market or for exports.

There was also an important difference from the period of recovery in the mid-1970s: then, Latin America grew faster than the industrial countries, and particularly the USA, while in 1984 Latin America grew at a significantly slower rate than the USA (and at the same rate as the average for industrial countries).

The positive impact of the recovery in industrial countries (and particularly the USA) has therefore been weakened by a number of factors.

1. The most important factor seems to be the continued negative transfer of financial resources, which we have emphasized above. The recovery in the USA did not bring about a significant increase in credit flows to Latin America (on the contrary, the US growth, accompanied by high interest rates, seems to be attracting large flows to the USA from abroad, and, by providing a safer alternative to lending to developing countries, may to some extent have even discouraged lending to Latin America); nor has the recovery implied a significant reduction even in nominal interest rates. We have given above (Chapter 2) the magnitudes of the negative transfers of resources from Latin America as a whole; it is noteworthy that these transfers abroad in 1983–4 amounted to over 5 per cent of Brazil and Mexico's national incomes and almost 9 per cent of national income in the Chilean case!

2. The impact of the industrial countries' recovery on Latin American exports was mixed. On the one hand, Latin America (as well as most of the developing world) was able to increase the volume of its exports quite significantly. According to ECLAC,[8] the volume of Latin American exports grew by 8.6 per cent in 1983, and by 9.8 per cent in 1984; but it has been estimated that 85 per cent of the increase in Latin American exports was sold to the USA. However, on the other hand, the price of Latin American exports declined, significantly (by −8.1 per cent) in 1983, and marginally even in 1984 (by −0.5 per cent); Latin America's terms of trade declined by over 6 per cent in 1983 and improved very marginally (by 0.2 per cent) in 1984.

It is as yet unclear exactly why the 1983–4 industrial countries' recovery has not—as in the past—led to an improvement in the prices of commodities, and thus in Latin America's terms of trade. Part of the explanation seems to lie in the distribution of the recovery between the USA and the rest of the industrial world. As seen above, US growth was far higher than that of the rest of the industrial countries. The USA accounts for an important—but by no means predominant—part of commodity exports for developing countries; for example, in 1982, the USA bought 8.0 per cent of agricultural raw materials and 15.7 of ores and metals exported by the developing countries, whereas the rest of the market industrial economies bough 48 per cent of the former and 43 per cent of the latter, and other developing countries bought 31 per cent of the former and 25 per cent of the latter. Both Europe and Japan are more important markets for developing countries than the USA for all commodity groups other than manufactures.[9] Thus, although the US recovery was large, its impact, particularly on demand for primary commodities, was relatively small; a far larger positive trade effect was exerted by the expansion of the USA on exporters of manufactured goods. Another factor that may have reduced the positive impact of industrial countries' recovery on Latin America's terms of trade is linked to the previously discussed need for many developing countries either to generate large trade surpluses (as in Latin America) or, in the case of non-Latin American countries, substantially to reduce trade deficits, due in both cases to sharp declines in net transfer of financial flows to them. If many developing countries simultaneously attempt significantly to increase the volume of their exports of commodities, there can be a downward pressure on those countries' terms of trade as the price of their commodities fall; if demand is very price-inelastic and the supply increase very large, the value of their exports could even decline, in what Bhagwati has characterized as 'inmiserizing growth'. Thus, the weakness of commodity prices in the current recovery may be related to this over-supply of commodities caused by many exporters simultaneously seeking to adjust their economy.

There is further important difference with the mid-1970s recovery, when most developing countries grew faster than the industrial ones, and when, largely related to this, inter-developing-country trade expanded very rapidly.[10] On the contrary, as developing countries in 1983–4 saw their output fall, or grow less than that of industrial countries, and as the level of their total imports was reduced in 1984 below previous levels, inter-developing-countries' trade ceased to be a dynamic source of demand for Latin

American exports. There is also some evidence that low inflation and particularly high real interest rates have significantly reduced the demand for stocks of commodities, as holding more liquid assets becomes significantly more attractive. Last but not least, policies of industrial countries in their own agricultural sector, technological changes, and increased protectionism seem to imply a structural decline in the international demand for many of the commodities exported by Latin America.

A final caveat seems necessary. It has been argued[11] that increases in the value of exports, as occurred in Latin America in 1984 as a result of the industrial countries' recovery, have 'compensated' developing countries for the high interest rates at which they have to service their debt. As Dornbusch[12] clearly points out, when the increase in exports is explained exclusively by a larger volume of exports (as was the Latin American experience in 1984), such statements are clearly incorrect in terms of welfare economic theory. If terms of trade do not improve, a high level of debt servicing, provided by increased volumes of exports, implies that the Latin American economies are shifting their own rsources into exports by sacrificing domestic absorption, either in consumption or investment; this additional production effort does not have any positive counterpart for Latin Americans, as it is used up to sustain high levels of debt servicing.

Looking through the crystal ball

There is a large literature on forecasting different scenarios for Latin American balance of payments and growth up to the 1990s.[13] We will not attempt to add another scenario, but will briefly point out the problematic features, implicit or explicit, in even the more optimistic forecasts.

First, it must be stressed that most 'scenario builders' focus on whether the debt problem will be manageable in the late 1980s, as reflected in a reduction of debt service and debt/export ratios. They are thus basically concerned whether the debt crises will be overcome mainly for the benefit of the international banks' stability; the argument that this will also imply an improvement of developing countries' 'creditworthiness' is a weak one. As we have pointed out above, there is no evidence that such an improvement would lead to the only benefit which such countries could expect from it—that is, greatly enhanced and stable flows of external finance at a reasonable cost. The concern whether the crises of national development and growth will be overcome is clearly secondary in most of these projections.

These forecasts show that *if* a number of rather doubtful pre-conditions are *simultaneously met*, then the debt/exports ratio can decline rather significantly by the end of the decade. Amongst the most problematic assumptions that characterize most of those optimistic forecasts is that industrial countries' annual growth averages around 3 per cent or more for the rest of the decade (and does so without major cyclical variations); that protectionism does not intensify in the industrial countries; that interest rates decline in real and nominal terms; and that there are no unforeseen new major shocks for the rest of the decade (such as violent fluctuations of oil prices, interest rates, or exchange rates).

As we discussed in the previous chapter, there are structural features which seem to inhibit sustained growth in industrial countries. These long-term problems are clearly currently accentuated by the unbalanced and precarious nature of US growth.

In 1985, the US economy slowed down, to levels well below the growth that had been forecast. In the first quarter of 1985, growth in GDP of *only* 0.7 per cent was well below the levels widely forecast (for example, the OECD had been projecting 2.75 per cent for the first half of 1985, and other, particularly US government, sources were far more optimistic) and far beneath the 6.75 per cent growth of US GNP during the whole of 1984. The decline in US growth is explained not by a reduction of total aggregate demand, which was still growing quite rapidly in early 1985, but by the fact that a high proportion of this increased demand was met by the surging level of imports, which helps explain the mounting US trade deficit. Fears have been expressed that, if the US government does effectively reduce the huge US budget deficit, this might occur at a time when the US and world economic activities were moving into a cyclical recession; thus, because of the time-lags involved, the US economy could be caught in a double squeeze between depressed domestic demand and the continued leakage into imports.

To this risk is added the fear that the size of US current account deficits, the slowing down of the US economy or other unexpected factors could cause the value of the dollar to decline sharply, and that this would provoke the US government into restrictive policies leading to higher interest rates, so as to prevent the reacceleration of inflation.[14] The fact that this type of scenario is openly discussed in the international financial press as a possibility should be a cause of concern. For example, in an article in *The Financial Times*, Max Wilkinson writes:[15]

At the worst, it is possible to envisage a collapse of world trade at the same time as inflationary pressures kept nominal interest rates at high levels. This would badly damage the ability of Latin American and other Third World debtor countries to service their debts and could even precipitate the long feared world banking crisis.

(This scenario may be excessively pessimistic, as it does not mention the positive impact that a decline in the value of the dollar would have on the real value of the debt.)

A second cause of concern is the unwillingness of the other industrial countries (and particularly of those with large current account surpluses and low rates of inflation) to undertake more reflationary policies—and thus compensate for the rapid deceleration in US growth, which may be reinforced if effective measures are taken to reduce the US budget deficit. The major dilemma is as follows. On the one hand, rapid but unbalanced growth, mainly by the USA (with huge US budget and trade deficits, as well as large capital inflows from abroad) is unsustainable in the medium term, as it would lead to extremely high levels of net US debt, and such growth may already be petering out. On the other hand, if the USA stops playing the 'locomotive' role, as it did in 1983, and particularly in 1984, and if other industrial countries are unwilling to replace it in such a role, industrial countries' growth could decline significantly, dragging down the rest of the world economy with them.

The other clear danger that challenges the feasibility of optimistic scenarios is that the very success of developing countries' export strategies—required to generate the trade surpluses necessary to make the debt problem manageable—will become increasingly unacceptable to industrial countries' workers and entrepreneurs. As a result, there is an important danger that existing pressure for increased protectionism will intensify, and will have a stronger impact than hitherto on government policies, particularly in the USA. Serious consideration by the US Congress of a uniform import surcharge is one important indicator of the threat posed by increased protectionism. Concrete action by the Reagan administration against particular countries, aimed apparently at preventing such a generalized move by Congress, attests to the seriousness of the threat.

Factors that slowed down growth in Latin America in 1983–4 are likely to continue to operate broadly in the same direction. For example the reasons given above for continued weak prices of commodities would seem to continue to be applicable; unless unforeseen events occur, it would seem that the price of most commodities will not increase significantly in the near future.

There are therefore very serious risks that changes in the international environment may imply that a continued management of debt crises is not feasible unless even greater austerity is extracted from LDCs—a situation that is becoming increasingly untenable after years of growing unemployment, and stagnating or falling real per capita incomes and wages.

The second—and, from our perspective, the key—problem of the optimistic scenarios is that, even *if* all or most of the assumptions held (which, as we saw above, is rather unlikely), 'satisfactory' management of the debt crisis would continue to require Latin American countries during the rest of the decade at least to serve the interest on the debt, which they are only partially able to do, thus continuing their net negative transfer of financial resources abroad, particularly to the USA and mostly to only eight banks. For example, Enders and Mattione[16] projected that less than one-quarter of the continent's interest payments would be covered by new loans between 1983 and 1987, and that there would be a net transfer of resources of roughly US $150 billion from the region during that period. Although accepting that 'it is true that the normal flow of capital is from developed to developing countries', Cline forecasts that 'for most of the 1980's the interest due on past debt is likely to exceed net new capital inflows'![17]

To sustain such levels of resource transfers and trade surpluses, the IMF in its 1984 *World Economic Outlook* projects that the volume of imports of the major borrowers would not exceed their 1981 levels until 1987 and, in respect of the net oil exporters, until 1988. Professor Cline's optimistic projections imply that per capita GNP in the larger Latin American countries would in 1990 barely exceed its 1980 level; he therefore concludes that, according to his projections, '*the 1980's as a whole seem likely to be a lost decade in terms of economic growth* for the major debtor countries that have been in debt servicing difficulties' (our emphasis). It seems worth emphasizing that Cline's projections are amongst the most optimistic ones: for example, the Enders and Mattione study quoted above had an even lower forecast for GDP growth in Latin America after 1983 than did Professor Cline's study.

An Inter-American Development Bank study,[18] with different and more pessimistic assumptions than the Cline model, asks the far more central question of whether, with existing trends, higher GNP growth for Latin America can be sustained (this study assumes a growth rate of around 5 per cent for Latin America for 1985–8); the result of the projection is that such growth would be unsustainable because of the impossibility of covering the financing gap of the resulting external deficits.

The conclusion must therefore be that the circle cannot be squared, and that it seems very unlikely that, simultaneously, meaningful growth will be restored in Latin America and the countries of the region will be able to continue to 'manage' their debt problem, unless major structural changes are introduced both in the Latin American development strategies, in the international financial system, and in the policies of major industrial countries, particularly the USA. If major changes are not introduced, there is the risk that debt crises will continue, and probably worsen to default situations, at the same time as Latin America continues to stagnate.

Fundamental changes, both in the international financial system and in countries' development strategies, are therefore urgently required, so as to overcome the vicious circle of debt crises and stagnation which has haunted Latin America since the early 1980s. As we will argue in the next chapter, for major changes to occur—both nationally and internationally—Latin American governments would have to play a leading role in bringing them about, as creditor governments and institutions will only accept major changes under pressure.

Under these circumstances, the question is not really whether industrial countries, and particularly the USA, will assume part of the costs of solving the debt crisis: given foreseeable conditions, they will inevitably have to do so. The real question is not *whether*, but *when* and *how* the USA and other industrial countries will intervene, before or after the breakdown of crisis management; *ex ante*, in order to prevent the breakdown, or *ex post*, in order to try to pick up the pieces. The urgent task for all governments concerned, particularly the USA, the international institutions, and transnational banks, is to move from an unsustainable debt management scenario to a resumption of a growth and development scenario, in order to avoid the catastrophic picture of current projections.

Notes

1. See, for example, P. Montagnon, 'Debt Crisis: Euphoria Fades as Problem Remains Acute', *Financial Times*, 18 March 1985, International Capital Markets Supplement; and P. Montagnon, 'The International Debt Problem: Beset with Setbacks on Several Fronts', *Financial Times*, 7 May 1983, World Banking Supplement.
2. IMF, *World Economic Outlook*, Washington, DC, 1984.
3. W. Cline, *International Debt, Systemic Risk and Policy Response*, Cambridge, Mass., 1984, p. 199.
4. See, for example, IMF Occasional Paper 31, *International Capital Markets, Developments and Prospects*, Washington, DC, August 1984.
5. A Fishlow, 'The Debt Crisis: Round Two Ahead?', in R. Feinberg and V. Kallab, eds., *Adjustment Crisis in the Third World*, Cambridge, Mass., 1984.
6. For a very clear discussion of these possibilities, see D. Lessard and J. Williamson, *Financial Intermediation Beyond the Debt Crisis*, Washington, DC, September 1985.
7. OECD, *Economic Outlook* 36, December 1984.
8. ECLAC, *Preliminary Overview of the Latin American Economy During 1984*.
9. UNCTAD, *Trade and Development Report 1984*, part 1.
10. See, for example, S. Griffith-Jones and C. Harvey, eds., *World Prices and Development*, Gower, London, 1985.
11. See, for example, Ronald Reagan's IMF address, in *New York Times*, 26 September 1984, for a clear statement of this position.
12. R. Dornbusch, *The Effects of OECD Macro-economic Policies on Non-oil LDCs: A Review*, September 1984, mimeo, Massachusetts Institute of Technology.
13. For useful summaries, see Cline, *International Debt* . . . and Commonwealth Secretariat, *The Debt Crises and the World Economy*

(widely known as 'The Lever Report'), London, 1984, particularly Ch. 5 and Appendix 5.1.

14. This risk is discussed in S. Marris, *Dollars and Deficits: The World Economy at Risk*, Washington, DC, 1985.

15. 'The World Economy: US Problems Remain Central', *Financial Times*, 7 May 1985, World Banking Supplement.

16. T. Enders and R. Mattione, *Latin America: The Crisis of Debt and Growth*, Washington, DC, 1984.

17. Cline, *International Debt* . . . .

18. Inter-American Development Bank, *Economic and Social Progress in Latin America*, Washington, DC, 1984.

CHAPTER 10

The Search for a New International Financial System

Introduction

As we have shown in the previous chapter, debt crisis management, as practised in recent years, has been successful only in one fundamental aspect: it has contributed towards avoiding—until now at least—any major threat to the stability of the international banks. Thus, although it has been to some extent problematic for the creditor banks and governments of industrial countries, debt crisis management has broadly served their main *short-term* aims, even though the medium-term concern with the banks' stability remains. From the point of view of the governments of debtor developing countries (and particularly the Latin American ones), debt crisis management has been fundamentally unsatisfactory, as it has not contributed towards sustaining, far less increasing, growth and development (see Chapters 2, 8, and 9). The burden of debt servicing on Latin American economies in recent years and in future ones (after the reschedulings were carried out) is still clearly inconsistent with rapid economic growth.

There has been increasing debate on the need to pass from debt crisis management to the search for more fundamental transformations in the international financial system, transformations that would make the current debt crisis less damaging, particularly to developing countries, and that would make future debt crises less likely, and less damaging to all parties involved.

In the last section of this chapter, we shall review the main schemes that have been suggested for dealing in a more fundamental way with the debt crisis, and for designing a more appropriate system of international financial intermediation for the future. As will become very apparent from our review, there is no shortage of interesting ideas for dealing with the problems posed by the debt crises.

Has the time come for a debtors' initiative?

The fundamental problem, which we will address first, is the lack of willingness by creditors' governments and institutions to take any major initiative, and lack of sufficient pressure from debtor governments to use their new but unexploited bargaining strength for demanding such major changes.

It is true that an optimum approach for major changes in the international financial system would rely on multilateral arrangements negotiated between banks, their host governments, international financial institutions, and debtor governments. Supporters of such an approach[1] argue correctly that stability of the banking system and of sustained net financial flows to developing countries are a 'public good', too risky and too fraught with externalities to be provided by individual agents acting alone; furthermore, they argue that widespread debt crises are a 'public evil'. As a consequence, 'public problems seem to require public multilateral solutions'.

It seems increasingly evident—though extremely unfortunate —that in the current climate of opinion, *unless* major threats to the stability of the international banking system actually arise, creditor institutions and governments will make only relatively marginal concessions to debtors and only minor changes to the international financial system.

As a perceptive observer, A. Kaletsky[2] has clearly put it:

It would be possible in theory for a solution to be reached without the disruption of a default. In reality, however, an immediate leap from the current ad hoc reschedulings, based on market interest rates and traditional banking arrangements, to an 'agreed default' is not very plausible . . . *It is probable, therefore, that debtors will have to take the law into their own hands if they want any substantial relief from their present financial constraints.* (Our emphasis.)

Paradoxically, such action, by Latin American debtors in particular, is made easier by the fact that their bargaining strength was significantly enhanced by the recent changes in the international environment, which have meant that these countries have become net exporters of financial resources. As we pointed out above, when net transfers of financial resources flow towards a developing country, the greater bargaining strength lies with the lender, as it is he who must ultimately decide to make the new loans, and take concrete action so as to transfer the funds; as a result, the lender can easily impose all types of conditions. When there are, however, negative financial flows from a country or a region, the greater bargaining strength has potentially shifted to the debtor government or governments, as it is they who must decide to repay and ultimately take the action of actually transferring the funds. As a result, the debtor is potentially —if he uses his bargaining strength appropriately and fully— in the position not only to resist the conditions of the lender but, much more fundamentally, to impose his own. We believe this shift in bargaining strength has not as yet been fully perceived by all debtor governments.

As Krugman's[3] model shows, when net transfers are negative, there is a range of possible outcomes of negotiations between creditors and debtors, between the point of 'minimal' rescheduling (which gives the debtor just enough not to provoke default) and 'maximal' rescheduling, which is just short of making creditors unwilling to continue lending to avert default. Krugman concludes that the recent management of the debt crisis, for example, for the three major Latin American debtors, entailing such major resource transfers *from* them, has implied 'a pretty good bargain for the creditors in the short run, while pursuing the possibility of eventual normal servicing of the debt in the longer run'. This conclusion is based on the assumption which Krugman derives from his theoretical analysis, but which he argues is in any case obvious, that 'lending to a debtor to avoid immediate default is always worthwhile as long as the new lending is less than the debt service'.

Given the 'substantial unexploited bargaining potential' that Latin American governments (at least in theory) seem to possess, it seems crucial for them radically to redefine the 'minimum' deal that is acceptable to them in bargaining on debt reschedulings and new flows. Clearly, such a minimum cannot be defined in the abstract, but must be consistent with acceptable 'minimum' levels of growth for the debtor economies, and consistent with acceptable levels of employment, as well as acceptable levels of income, for the majority of the people.

While large negative net transfers from Latin American economies persist, their governments are faced with an impossible dilemma. They either reduce their level of investment significantly[4] or they increase their savings to levels well beyond those politically feasible, particularly in countries returning to democratic systems. As we have shown, continued negative net transfers of financial resources abroad are clearly incompatible with sustained growth. Consequently, resistance by debtor governments to such transfers will increase significantly, and may at some point even cause an outright default or repudiation of the total debt, with very harmful effects both for the stability of the banks and for the world economy as a whole. In its turn, the possibility of such defaults make banks unwilling to increase their new lending, prolonging and aggravating the situation of negative net transfers, until major changes are introduced. Radical Latin American politicians and academics are indeed increasingly suggesting almost the likelihood of such a course of action. For example, Fidel Castro, in a major interview devoted mainly to the subject of Latin America's foreign debt, concludes:

the ideal, most constructive thing is for these problems [of debt overhang] to be solved by means of political dialogue and negotiation, which would promote essential solutions in an orderly manner. If this is not done, desperate situations will doubtless force a group of countries to take unilateral measures. This isn't desirable, but, if it occurs, I am sure that all other countries in Latin America and the rest of the Third World will join them.[5]

To a certain extent, unilateral actions from debtor countries have already begun, with the Peruvian government's step to limit debt service payments to 10 per cent of exports. In announcing this measure, the Peruvian president, Alan Garcia (whose ideology is by no means a revolutionary one), stated that 'the first creditor of Peru is its people'. Similar statements (although not yet actions) have come from other Latin American political leaders.

Furthermore, some broad radical proposals have begun to emerge that would reduce the debt burden in a context of enhanced development. For example, Sunkel[6] has suggested that part or all of debt servicing could be made in local currency and devoted to investment in development projects, following rigorous and clearly established public criteria, negotiated between governments of industrial and developing countries, and monitored by international development agencies. It is noteworthy that Ortiz Mena, the President of the Inter-American Development Bank, was reported to have endorsed a similar proposal.[7]

As Kaletsky has pointed out,[8] there seems to be a range of intermediate options for debtors between outright default—so disruptive to the stability of the international banking system—and continuation of current debt crisis management—so harmful to debtors' growth prospects. Such intermediate options (called by Kaletsky a 'conciliatory default', but which we would, even more moderately, call a 'conciliatory medium-term moratorium') would have the advantage of being drastic enough to change significantly the framework for bargaining without being so drastic as to endanger the stability of the international banks.

In practical terms, such an approach could be implemented if, for example, debtor governments (individually or collectively) suspended negative net transfers of financial resources during the next few years (for example, for the next three to five years), while clearly committing themselves to servicing their debt in the long term. In fact, the suspension of negative net transfers would be justified on the basis not only of the need to allow for growth in the national economies for the sake of its people, but also of the need for strengthening the country's long-term capacity to service its debt. Furthermore, it is evident that more rapid growth in debtor countries would be of benefit to exporters from industrial countries. Undoubtedly, some additional public funds from industrial countries, as well as to multinationals with investments in those countries' governments would be required, but the amounts involved would be small in relation to the potential cost of an outright default.

A unilateral declaration of cessation of negative net transfers would imply that governments would continue servicing the debt to the equivalent level at which the country is obtaining new capital flows. Consequently, if new credits increased, so would the volume of debt servicing. Such a bargaining position would imply a strong incentive for creditor governments and/or international financial institutions to expand their direct lending or their guarantees, or an incentive for the creation of international liquidity (for example, by a new issue of SDR's). Furthermore, the elimination of negative net transfers could be made consistent with one or—more probably—with a combination of the types of proposal already being discussed amongst industrial countries' central and private bankers (see review in this chapter). The private banks would exert strong pressure for such new flows or changes to occur, as they would have a clear vested interest in them.[9] As a result, debtor developing countries would find powerful allies explicitly on their side! Furthermore, servicing at market rates could be restored earlier than the three- to five-year period initially announced, not only if new flows were significant, but also if international interest rates declined significantly or world trade rose very rapidly.

A proposal which attempts to eliminate negative transfers from developing countries so as to sustain those countries' development may seem perhaps too radical. However, a major Commonwealth Secretariat Report on the subject (see note 1 to this chapter) has already stated that 'any satisfactory solution to the present situation must as a matter of urgency put an end to the premature outflow of resources from developing countries. There must be an end to premature negative transfers of resources and the quest for developing country trade surpluses'. Somewhat more surprisingly, in a recent publication of Business Latin America,[10] an organization representing the largest multinational companies doing business in and with the continent, follows a similar line. It says that action is 'definitely needed to offset the potentially destabilizing impact of the debt crisis on fragile democratic structures. . . . The current approach means that real growth in Latin America is being sacrificed to meet immediate debt-service requirements'.

Although the choice of the package of mechanisms to channel new funds or reduce debt obligations would basically be left to the creditors (and would probably be guided largely by their need to avoid damage to the stability of major international banks), the measures which would be likely to emerge—new issue of SDRs, for example—would in fact not only benefit the debtor economies, but would also have a potentially beneficial medium-term effect on the world economy. The use of 'debtor power' would, for example, force public international institutions to play a larger role in the world financial system, which economists as distinguished as Keynes and Triffin have for a long time argued (see Chapter 3) would make the system stronger and more stable.

The optimum outcome would occur if the measures initially sparked off by such a semi-emergency situation were later consolidated by other reforms into a system that would generate predictable, supervised, and appropriate net flows to developing countries. We further believe that the resulting shift towards greater public control of the international financial system, whose uncontrolled privatization during the 1970s was an important factor leading to the debt crisis of the 1980s, would imply an extremely positive reversal of power to governments, both in industrial and in developing countries. It would not be the first time in the history of international economic relations that major institutional improvements would be the final outcome of a crisis. (The advantage of the path proposed is that the crisis would be regulated, so that the worst negative impacts could be avoided, for the benefit of all the different actors involved.)

To make conciliatory moratoria consistent with the main target that justifies such actions by debtor countries—their growth and development—this measure should be placed in the context of an explicit development strategy, which would guarantee that the additional foreign exchange retained in the country would be productively used (for example, via a Special Development Fund), and that the broad strategy adopted would be such as to make future debt crises less likely to recur (for example, by declining reliance in future on foreign savings).

The development strategy (and particularly the use of the funds corresponding to reductions of debt servicing) would be set in the framework of clear development criteria, such as generation of new employment, production of goods and services essential to the welfare of the majorities, and generation of additional foreign exchange via export promotion and/or import substitution.

As there would be a very radical change to a far greater emphasis on medium-term growth, and long-term development, current procedures for monitoring countries' performance, which rely excessively on the Fund's role and on short-term stabilization, would have to be significantly modified to suit the new perspective. This would imply, not a weakening of international monitoring, but a change in its nature. Such monitoring could be carried out by, for example, what Gustav Ranis has called a Country Resource and Assessment Commission, to be comprised of representatives from the country, representatives from other third world countries, and outside independent experts, as well as representatives of official international institutions, (with a far greater emphasis on the role to be played by those institutions concerned with development, such as the World Bank, the regional development banks, and UNCTAD, and with a relatively smaller role played by the IMF in this monitoring). Such a committee would evaluate and monitor progress both in short-term stabilization and in development, with emphasis on medium-term sustained and equitable growth. It is noteworthy that such an approach was quite successfully implemented during the operation of the Alliance for Progress in the 1960s, when a 'Committee of Wise Men'—largely drawn from internationally recognized independent experts, including several from Latin America countries— monitored countries' progress in their development plans as a precondition for obtaining US aid flows. To a certain extent, precedents also exist in the role that the World Bank has played in relation to aid consortia, for example, for countries like India. In those cases, debt rescheduling and new flows have been simultaneously discussed in the framework of a medium-term development programme.

Though stabilization would inevitably continue to be a very major concern, the emphasis of monitoring would, it is hoped, shift to expansionary and equitable stabilization, within the framework of a medium-term development plan.[11] Although inevitable difficulties would arise, extreme misuse of funds from a developmental point of view—for example, the major capital flights and import sprees which have characterized several important Latin American countries since the mid-1970s, and were made possible by excessive abundance of funds and the almost total lack of supervision of their use—could largely be avoided by appropriate and fairly rigorous national and international monitoring (such as has always existed to an important extent in the monitoring of aid flows).

A final caveat seems essential. A larger potential for significant improvement in treatment from the international financial community is feasible for large bank debtors, which tend also to have large negative net transfers at present. However, it seems to us incorrect to argue, as many analysts have done, that the debt problem is primarily one of large debtors (and mainly Latin American ones). Debt crises in low-income countries (and particularly sub-Saharan ones) began even earlier, are even more damaging to those countries' economies, and cause even greater hardship.[12] If the large debtors *do* use their unexploited bargaining strength to get a better deal for themselves, it is to be hoped that they do so in a context which improves—or at the very least does not damage—the net transfer of financial flows to the needy low-income countries. In this sense it is a cause of concern that, as reported in the April 1985 IMF *World Economic Outlook*, the trend since 1981 has been that, while net disbursements from official creditors remained fairly stable in nominal terms, the share of these flows going to middle-income economies, often in the context of 'concerted lending' and rescheduling packages, linked to their debt crises, has increased significantly; as a result, net official flows to low-income countries have been to a certain extent 'crowded out', as those countries received in 1983–4 lower nominal net official flows than they were getting in 1979–80. In this sense, measures that benefit all developing countries—although far more difficult to achieve—would imply a far greater level of equity than would be ensured either by the case-by-case approach or agreements with particular categories of debtors.

Issues raised by the debt crisis of the 1980s

In the final section of this chapter, we will attempt an evaluation of the different proposals made in different circles to deal with the debt crisis, and with the problem of future financial flows to developing countries. Before doings so, we wish briefly to summarize what we see as the main problems raised by the debt crisis of the 1980s, to be addressed by any major modification of the international financial system that would deal in a fundamental manner with these problems. The problems, although related, are analytically clearly separate.

A first problem broadly recognized was the liquidity crisis of developing countries, which meant their inability to service and amortize debts in the short term within the time schedule and in the full amounts initially contracted. The liquidity problem was intimately linked to the dramatic changes in the net basic transfer of flows which we have described above for Latin America (see, in particular, the first section of Chapter 8). Other developing countries have faced a sharp decline in their net transfers, even though these flows remained positive. For example, low-income African countries saw the level of net transfers to them decline (in nominal terms) by 30 per cent during 1981 and by around 35 per cent in 1982. Continued negative net transfers of financial resources in Latin America have been a major factor contributing to a reversal of previously uninterrupted growth. Similarly, the drastic decline in net transfers to sub-Saharan Africa has provided an important additional constraint on an already extremely severe—and often critical—situation.

A second problem is that of equity in the current international management of debt crises. It is increasingly apparent that there has been an inequitable distribution of responsibility and costs between debtor countries, creditor country governments, and creditor private banks; given that responsibility for the debt crises is widely accepted as shared by all three agents, the burden of adjustment has been placed excessively on the debtor developing countries.

There is also the issue of the burden carried by different developing country debtors. As reschedulings have proceeded on a case-by-case basis (rather than according to some previously established criteria), some important differences have emerged in the terms and amount of the debt relief obtained, the size of the new lending linked to the rescheduling package, and the magnitude, as well as the type, of adjustment that has had to be accepted as a condition for the rescheduling and the new flows. These differences do not seem related to the level of countries' development or to their ability to pay or adjust.

It has also been argued that the adjustment does not imply an equitable sharing of the burden between different social groups. As, for example, Dornbusch and Diaz-Alejandro[13] have argued, while debt accumulation in several countries benefited mainly the upper middle classes who engaged in capital flight or the middle classes that enjoyed an import spree, the adjustment effort to service the debt falls largely on labour, via reduction of real wages and employment.

A third problem is the risk to the stability of the international banking system. Vulnerability in respect to developing-country lending is particularly dangerous at a time when some major banks are already suffering important losses in their domestic lending, and when bank bankruptcies have increased rapidly.

A fourth problem is the broader, medium-term issue of regenerating sustained positive transfers of capital to developing (and other) countries whose programmes of productive investment exceed their national savings. This issue is linked to two separate but related factors: (*a*) the creation of conditions and mechanisms to encourage new flows (particularly private ones), given that the economic agents which have been able to channel significant flows to developing countries in the past no longer seem to do so to the same extent; and (b) the creation of lending instruments more appropriate to development finance than the short-maturity, floating-interest credits which characterized such a high proportion of financial flows to developing countries in the 1970s.

Types of proposals for reform

Given the large number of proposals being reviewed here, we will attempt first to distinguish different categories amongst them, which seems essential for the evaluation that follows. A first distinction can be made between proposals that aim (1) to reduce or restructure the 'debt overhang', (2) to encourage new flows,and (3) to enhance the stability of the international banking system.

1. Schemes which attempt to reduce the impact of previously contracted debt can be subdivided into those which affect the level of the principal outstanding (as well as its amortization) and those which seek to affect the interest burden. Proposals to reduce the *level* of outstanding debt below its book value were emphasized far more in the very early stages of the post-1982 crisis (see below), as a first response to it, but they were not backed by government officials of industrial countries, nor by most private bankers; the bank debt crisis was not regarded by them as sufficiently acute to require such radical schemes. At a later stage, more limited proposals emerged to reduce the interest burden (in most schemes, temporarily), without affecting the value of outstanding debt. This type of proposal received important backing when—after significant rises in the US prime rate during the second quarter of 1984—senior US monetary officials proposed or discussed an interest 'cap'.

2. Schemes to encourage new private flows to developing countries, for example, via guarantees from industrial countries' governments, also received official support. Proposals to increase new public flows (via either existing or new public international institutions), although clearly continuing on the agenda of the Group of 24 (representing developing countries in monetary matters), seem at present to receive relatively little backing from industrial countries' governments.

These two approaches to the problem are clearly related, although they proceed from different directions. For example, continued failure to generate or encourage sufficient new lending to developing countries will decrease the ability and willingness of debtor governments to service their debts, thus probably revitalizing proposals for reducing the debt burden; for this reason 'overhang' proposals clearly need serious consideration. Several of the proposals discussed below (for example, those by Lord Lever and George Soros) attempt to address both problems simultaneously.

3. Closely related, but analytically separate, proposals are those which focus on the need to protect the stability of the banking system and of flows to developing countries, via an explicit clarification of the role of the Central Banks as international lenders of last resort, plus far tighter supervision. In times of recession or financial distress (like the period since 1982), such measures would encourage higher new flows, but in times of boom and euphoria (such as the late 1970s), new flows would be curtailed.

From another point of view, proposals relating to the debt crisis differ considerably according to which interests (those of creditor banks, debtor governments, creditor governments, exporters to developing countries) they would primarily serve. This distinction is relevant in itself, as well as in relation to the crucial issue of the potential backing that different proposals are likely to receive. A proposal would seem more likely to be implemented if it gathers support from specific influential interests (for example, large banks, major industrial country exporters, governments of major debtor countries) and does not generate too much opposition (does *not*, for instance, require too much actual or potential money from industrial countries' taxpayers). As discussed above, the optimum way in which major changes could be achieved would be through multilateral arrangements negotiated between banks, their host governments, official international institutions, and debtor governments.

A unilateral approach, although clearly a 'second best', will become increasingly relevant, as we have pointed out above, if the world economic environment does not alleviate the debt burden sufficiently, and/or significant measures are not taken by the markets, or by multilateral action, at least to eliminate negative net transfers very soon, and to aim to restore positive flows to developing countries. This approach implies unilateral action by one debtor or a collective, but not necessarily outright default.

Evaluation of different proposals

Given the large number of schemes that have been suggested, we concentrate more on those which are seen as more likely to attain the twin objectives of sustaining growth in developing countries (in the short and the long term) and improving the resilience of the international banking system. We will attempt to clarify not only the exact nature of the proposals, but also their objectives, their feasibility, their estimated cost, and their wider implications for the different agents involved in the debt crisis.

Adaptations to the current system

New SDR issue. A general form in which the external financial problems of all developing countries could be eased would be by a new issue of SDRs.[14] The case for this has received widespread support, based on evidence that, in the early 1980s, SDRs declined significantly as a proportion of non-gold reserves, and that, for most developing countries, the ratio between reserves and imports fell well below its level in the late 1970s. Furthermore, according to BIS figures, global non-gold reserves in 1983 were below their 1981 level. Also, in the context of the debt problem, it is particularly important that SDR allocations provide new liquidity, thus easing present foreign exchange constraints, *without* creating repayment obligations, and thus without generating future debt problems. Finally, an attractive feature of SDR allocations is that they do not require an expansion of Public Sector Borrowing Requirement (PSBR) of industrial countries, nor parliamentary approval by the member governments of the IMF (this is particularly relevant in the case of the US Congress).

More broadly, a new issue of SDRs would be an important step in reaffirming the dwindling role of this international currency in the world economy, in spite of a commitment to make it 'the main reserve currency'.

The increased role for public international creation of liquidity by official international institutions should inevitably become more crucial (and more feasible) as market generation of liquidity—so important in the 1970s—loses its relative importance.

The Search for a New System 145

Expansion and adaptation of existing compensatory financing facilities. The first change in the rules of the game that developing countries succeeded in securing was the introduction of the IMF Compensatory Financing Facility. A special IMF pamphlet spells out its main purpose:[15]

Ideally, the facility would enable a member to borrow when its export earnings are high and financial reserves are low and to repay when they are high, *so its import capacity is unaffected by fluctuations in export earnings caused by external events.* (Our emphasis.)

In the 1970s and early 1980s, the CFF became a major facility for providing payments assistance by the IMF to developing countries; however, borrowing under this facility remained rather modest, considering the terms of trade deterioration experienced by LDCs in the early 1980s. The main problems have been identified[16] as the quota limits on maximum drawings (the most important constraint), the calculation of export shortfalls in nominal terms, and the drawing up of a formula for repayments not linked to the recovery of export earnings. A number of analysts have suggested a liberalization of the CFF so as to provide full coverage of export shortfalls, basically by eliminating the link between the size of the drawing allowed and a percentage of the country's quota. The advantage of such a change would be that stabilizing export earnings would have a desirable impact both on developing countries and on the world economy, and would contribute significantly to breaking the vicious circles of poor trade performance and financial distress; both the stability of the international banking system and of developing countries' growth would be enhanced. The fundamental objection is that of cost, and the problem of safeguarding the liquidity of the IMF, were the CFF to be significantly expanded.

Linked specifically to the emergence of widespread debt crises, there arose in influential circles, including the Mexican government,[17] the proposal that the CFF could also provide loans to offset fluctuations in nominal interest payments. As pointed out in Chapter 8, such a broadening of the CFF would have the merit of bringing one of the key *new* sources of international economic instability (large fluctuations in interest rates) within a mechanism dealing with the more traditional sources of instability from export earnings. Conceptually, perhaps the most precise aim for a modified CFF would be to attempt to *stabilize countries' real import capacity*, and to compensate, in cases of balance of payments need, for fluctuations in export prices, import prices, and interest rates beyond the country's control. An expanded CFF would have the virtue of taking into account the different internationally determined variables which affect a country's capacity to import, and thus its extraordinary financial requirements; in this sense, it would seem conceptually superior to proposals such as interest capping, which implicitly assume that the rest of the international economic environment (for example, world inflation and terms of trade) remain unchanged.

The calculations for the estimated additional cost of an 'interest rate window' for the CFF are quite complex; only very rough magnitudes have been estimated (for example in the Lever Report, and by Cline), based exclusively on the variable interest debt. Such a definition would take account mainly of the needs of large debtors, neglecting the fact that even official flows are subject to some (albeit smaller) interest rate fluctuations. The magnitudes involved would also be crucially influenced by whether the expanded and modified CFF drawings continued to have quota-related limits and, if so, whether these were significantly higher than existing ones. If they were not significantly expanded or removed, the net cost of introducing an 'interest window' into the CFF would be relatively low, but its beneficial counter-cyclical effects would be equally small; if the quota limits were linked to liquidity availability in the Fund, there would be the danger (which we feel should be clearly avoided) that funds would be diverted from compensating for export fluctuations (mainly a low-income country problem) to compensating for interest rate fluctuations (clearly a more important problem for middle-income, large debtor countries). Therefore, it would seem vital to put the proposal in the context of an expansion of quota limits on drawings or, even better, of their removal. Clearly an expanded CFF, which would include compensation for interest rate increases, would give the IMF a broad capacity to finance temporary needs caused by international economic shocks; it would also provide significant counter-cyclical funding, crucial both to the LDCs affected and to the world economy.

The problem with an 'interest window', implying a large expansion, is its additional cost. A maximum limit is given by the variation of interest payments for all LDCs, excluding capital-surplus oil exporters (assuming debt outstanding is constant in nominal terms). Using World Bank figures[18] the largest such increase, between 1980 and 1981, reached the sum of US $4.2 billion for that one year. Such a figure could probably be accommodated with relative ease, particularly considering that not all countries with rising interest rate costs would have a balance of payments need. The main problem of cost would arise in periods such as the early 1980s, when real interest rates systematically rose; discounting the effect of the increase in the value of the debt, interest payments for all LDCs (except surplus oil exporters) rose by US $19.6 billion between 1978 and 1982.

Given the magnitudes involved, the issue of providing appropriate liquidity to the Fund for such an expanded and modified CFF would be crucial. An interesting idea suggested by William Cline is to use the emergency funding conditionally already available to the IMF through the significant expansion of the General Agreements to Borrow; in December 1983, the IMF had its lines of credit available from the GAB increased from SDR 6.4 billion to SDR 17 billion, to be used 'to forestall or cope with an impairment of the international monetary system'. If the participants in the GAB (the ten major industrial countries) were to authorize such a use, which would clearly be in the spirit, if not to the exact letter, of the expanded GAB, the initial liquidity problems for the IMF could be significantly reduced or even eliminated, without additional financial contributions from industrial countries. A very important problem would be that use of the GAB facility would seem to require high-conditionality, upper credit tranche arrangements with the IMF, whereas the CFF has up to now had relatively less stringent conditionality. Other funding possibilities would be finance by SDRs, funding by the IMF in the market, or possibly even quota expansion.

Two final caveats seem necessary on the subject of the CFF. First, its expansion—both conceptual and quantitative—does pose important problems. However, similar difficulties would be raised by other mechanisms to deal with the existing problems of instability in terms of trade, world inflation, and interest rates. The advantage of using the CFF would be that it is an existing mechanism and that, in spite of its limitations, previous experience with it has been positive. Given the current prevalence of institutional conservatism, the feasibility of expanding the CFF would seem relatively higher than other schemes (discussed below) with a greater element of institutional innovation.

A second caveat needs to be made about the assumptions on which the CFF's design was based. In the early 1960s, it was assumed, at that time correctly, that the main source of external instability for developing countries was the fluctuating value of their exports, which largely followed the cyclical pattern of activity in the industrial countries. A further important assumption was that these cycles of economic activity in industrial countries were short, and occurred within *a long-term trend of sustained growth*; this no longer seemed to hold true in the 1970s, and even less in the early 1980s. If stagnation or slow growth in the industrial countries were to persist for long periods, (which, as we discussed in Chapter 7, is clearly possible), perhaps an even more fundamental review of the CFF than has been suggested above might become necessary to reflect and incorporate the changing pattern of growth in the world economy. Were there to be, for example, a systematic trend toward decline in the terms of trade of all—or, more probably, of some—categories of developing countries and/or sustained high real interest rates, even a modified and expanded CFF would be insufficient to deal with those problems.

Interest 'capping' of various types. Alternative, or possibly complementary, forms of reducing interest payments—either temporarily or permanently—were proposed in 1984, under the general title of 'interest capping'. It is worth stressing that this idea has been raised or strongly supported by some of the most senior US monetary officials.[19] Debtor country governments, on the other hand, were less enthusiastic about such measures—even though they would clearly welcome them in the short term—because of their perception that they would 'have only limited utility since they simply postpone the problem' (Cartagena Declaration, June 1984).

Two different versions have been proposed: capping designed to stabilize interest payments over time (liquidity cap) and concessional capping. The liquidity cap would set a ceiling on interest rates on both new and rescheduled loans. If market rates rose above this ceiling, the difference would be added to the loan's principal due upon final maturity (that is, the increase in interest would be capitalized). If subsequently the market rate fell below the ceiling, the ceiling rate would continue to be paid and the difference deducted from the additional principal accumulated earlier. This liquidity cap would have considerable short-term advantages, in that it would provide essentially needed cash to developing countries, and would avoid unnecessary disruptions to their development and hardships to their population, because of temporary reductions of imports. It would imply a greater degree of equity than the current case-by-case approach to rescheduling, in that such a measure would follow a general rule, applicable to all countries with bank variable-interest borrowing—even though it would implicitly discriminate against those countries which did not wish, or were not able, to borrow on those terms in the past.

Several operational and institutional questions would need to be resolved before such a proposal could become a reality; bank regulators and accountants would have to be prepared to treat deferred interest favourably; an evaluation of potential negative stock market reaction to the implementation of such a proposal would be required, even though the negative reaction might be balanced by a perception that the interest cap significantly enhanced countries' willingness to service the debt in the medium term rather than take unilateral action. The key problem with the cap is that, *if* real interest rates were to remain high, the postponement of interest would merely transfer the problem into the future; in Dornbusch's words, it 'amounts to giving developing countries a credit card, not debt relief'. On the other hand, if real interest rates were low on average, a liquidity cap would provide timely and valuable temporary relief. Thus, a liquidity interest cap, accompanied by the adoption of policy measures in the main industrial countries conducive to a reduction in international real interest rates, would make an important contribution to relieving the short-term debt burden of LDCs and, indirectly, to increasing the stability of the international banking system.

While uncertainty remains about the future of interest rates, it may be desirable to consider the need for concessional capping.[20] Such concessionality would seem more feasible if it were temporary (for a period of three to five years, for example, as discussed above) and the cost shared by private banks and central banks. One possible mechanism would be for the difference between the market rate and the ceiling to be foregone, and the cost distributed amongst lower bank profits, plus a subsidy to the private banks from their central banks. This would imply a clear application of the principle of sharing costs of the debt crises amongst debtor countries, creditor governments, and creditor banks.

Let us estimate the implications of such concessionary capping for the largest US banks. According to Cline,[21] in 1982, the nine largest US banks had a gross pre-tax profit of US $5.5 billion, and total loans to non-oil LDCs and non-capital-surplus OPEC countries of US $78 billion. Each percentage of interest subsidy would have implied a maximum of US $780 million of cost, equivalent to approximately 14 per cent of the banks' total pre-tax earnings. A subsidy of 2 per cent would thus have implied a reduction of less than 30 per cent of their profits, which, though significant, would seem bearable. Were such a subsidy to be accompanied by one provided by the US Federal Reserve for an equivalent amount—US $1,560 million—a significant (4 per cent) reduction in interest rate cost would have been achieved without a disruptive impact on the banking system or a very significant expansion of the US money supply (compared, for example, with the cost of the Continental Illinois rescue). An undesirable effect would be that lower profits would imply a slower expansion of banks' capital, thus reducing the expansion of their ratio of capital to developing country assets, which banking regulators have tried to encourage. However, if a concessionary interest cap significantly increased the likelihood of repayment by LDCs (and thus the quality of the assets), such a move should be acceptable to bank regulators. A crucial problem would be which central bank would subsidize lending by non-US banks in dollars (the 'Fed', or the central bank in whose country the bank had its headquarters).

Compared with the CFF interest window proposal, and an interest cap which merely redistributes interest payments over time, a concessionary interest cap has the clear advantage of providing short-term relief to LDCs, *without* increasing the future debt burden.

If and when interest rates return to average lower levels, the possibility of using a liquidity cap for smoothing debt service payments would need to be examined. Lessard[22] and others have gone further to suggest the possibility of lending instruments where a real rate of interest would be contractually fixed, and the outstanding principal would be periodically adjusted for changes in some general price index. Although obviously attractive to LDC borrowers (in significantly reducing uncertainty concerning a major item of their balance of payments), it is unclear whether lenders can be found who are willing and able to carry out lending to LDCs on these terms. A further issue with index-linked debt is the choice of the index, particularly as the price index affecting the LDC (via its exports and imports) can differ significantly from the overall price index in the industrial country in whose currency the debt is denominated.

Internalizing debt-servicing obligations. An interesting variation on the 'interest cap' approach discussed was suggested by two ECLAC economists;[23] like the interest cap, this variation assumes a 'reference' interest rate, which in this proposal is equivalent to the long-term average of real international interest rates plus 'average spreads'. If the market rate is higher than the reference one, national debtors pay the total market interest to their Central Bank, which pays the creditors only up to the 'reference rate'; if, at a later period, the market rate is below the reference one, the Central Bank will draw on existing accumulated national currency to pay the reference rate (the Central Bank assuming the exchange rate risk, although not the commercial one). The advantage over the interest cap would be that the existence of funds in national currencies could provide a better guarantee of future repayments to international banks and their regulators than a mere commitment to pay.

Increasing repayment flexibility. Another approach attempts to adapt countries' servicing of debt to their 'ability to pay'. One mechanism would be to introduce 'bisque clauses' in lending arrangments (either existing or new ones), which would allow governments to defer part of repayment instalments, because of changed conditions, so that these could be repaid when the original maturity expired; such arrangements could be linked to clauses implying acceleration of repayment when the situation was more favourable than anticipated.[24] Obviously the flexibility would have to be clearly limited, so as to avoid becoming non-enforceable.

A number of proposals have been made to link debt service payments explicitly to the ability to pay, by fixing a maximum limit on the proportion of countries' foreign exchange earnings which would be devoted to servicing the debt. For example, the Cartagena Consensus suggests that 'external debt service must not engage export earnings beyond reasonable limits'. This document puts forward some rather general criteria for determining a limit 'compatible with sustaining adequate levels of domestic productive activity, always taking account of the particular features of each country's economy'. The Latin American institution, SELA (Sistema Economico para America Latina), in its 1984 *Study on Proposals for the Implementation of the Quito Declaration and Plan of Action*, suggested a maximum limit of 20 per cent of exports to be allocated for debt service. Bailey[25] and others have proposed linking debt amortization to countries' foreign exchange earnings (thus including sources of earnings such as workers' remittances). These concepts imply a welcome increase in risk-sharing between lenders and creditors; the higher the exports, the higher the servicing of the debt. This is attractive for debtor countries in that it makes debt servicing more counter-cyclical. It may be problematic for lenders in the same way as fixed interest lending would be—or more so.

Improving terms of debt rescheduling. If new financial flows to developing countries (from both private and official sources) were readily available, more equitable and possibly more efficient solutions to their external financing problems would be mainly achieved by new flows rather than relieving the most heavily indebted countries of part of their debt servicing. However, as new flows are very scarce and often linked to rescheduling packages, while net transfers have been declining and are in many cases negative, higher debt relief becomes extremely valuable and important.

Related—but sometimes clearly separate—issues arise from private bank debt rescheduling and the Paris Club reschedulings of official debt. In both cases, debtor governments—as well as institutions like UNCTAD[26]—have requested longer consolidation, grace, and maturity periods; they have also emphasized the significance of discussing new flows in the same, or related, fora in which reschedulings are agreed.

Although debt reschedulings have a long history (the Paris Club first met in 1956), the large number of countries and the vast sums of debt rescheduled since the early 1980s are a new phenomenon. There is as yet insufficient knowledge of the exact terms obtained by different countries and the factors which determine the differences in terms.

There are even basic problems of information on rescheduling. For example, interest rates on official debt, agreed bilaterally after the Paris Club meetings, are never published; in fact, the practices and procedures followed by creditor countries in determining these interest rates are rather obscure. Similarly, many debtor governments often have not even an approximate idea of the magnitude of their outstanding debt; this is particularly true of certain types of debt, such as open-book credit provided by suppliers.

Secondly, some countries have already been granted rather more favourable terms in their reschedulings on an *ad hoc* basis. Mexico and others obtained a multi-year rescheduling with private banks. Some low-income African countries have recently obtained quite generous terms; for example, Sudan, both in 1983 and 1984, obtained a debt rescheduling covering 100 per cent of its debt due in those years, with grace periods of over six years and with a total maturity of sixteen years or more; Madagascar obtained almost equally generous terms.[27] It would be interesting to evaluate the extent to which these more favourable terms enhanced growth and development, and the cost to creditors of the more generous reschedulings. This could provide valuable evidence of the impact which reform proposals would have if applied more widely to all countries seeking to reschedule their debt.

A final point seems relevant here. Although the measures discussed here are relatively minor, and above all would not require major institutional adaptation, the adoption of *several* of them would imply a rather significant change in the magnitude and even direction of net international flows to LDCs. Therefore, too sharp a distinction between 'minor changes' and 'fundamental reforms' seems analytically incorrect, particularly as the undertaking of several relatively minor changes may imply the first steps towards more fundamental reform; furthermore, such sharp distinctions may unnecessarily polarize debates on changes in the international monetary system.

More fundamental reforms

Many analysts have stressed the need for more fundamental reforms. These views are all based on the perception of major gaps and distortions in the existing structure of international lending to developing countries, and of recent severe discontinuities in the normal operation of international capital markets; they also take into account a perception that the growth of industrial economies and of world trade will not return to its post-war dynamism, and that a less favourable international environment will imply the need for a different structure of international financial flows. We shall distinguish three categories of proposals: those destined (i) to encourage new private credit flows, (ii) to enhance the stability of the international banking system and of the flows of private lending to LDCs, and (iii) to reduce the 'debt overhang'.

(i) *Encouragement of new private loans*. Much attention has been devoted to the creation of mechanisms which would provide insurance or guarantees for new loans. Several proposals seem broadly based on an extension of the principle applied by existing export credit guarantee insurance to cover bank lending to LDCs, not directly tied to particular goods or projects. As we shall see, most of the proposals give an important role to the Bretton Woods institutions, and attempt to avoid the creation of new institutions; Bolin and Del Canto[28] summarize the attitude shared by many of those making proposals in this field, in saying: 'the world doesn't need another public or private bureaucracy to increase loan activity—just a different balance sheet'.

A recent paper by Henry Wallich[29] discussed different options for insurance of bank lending to LDCs. The stated objectives are 'both to encourage LDC lending and to increase the safety of banks'. The problem faced is clearly stated: 'Continued lending, although on a more moderate scale is necessary for the good functioning of the world economy and the health of the international monetary system. Banks, especially smaller ones, feel considerable reluctance in that regard. Insurance may ease this problem.'

The Wallich paper favours the insurance of total portfolios (rather than particular loans) up to some fraction, the latter feature introducing an important element of co-insurance. The crucial issue of the proportion of the portfolio to be insured is discussed, but no figure is chosen; on the assumption that banking risk is modest, a suggestion for insuring 2 per cent of banks' loan portfolio is made. The assumption of risk behind that figure seems excessively conservative. Of perhaps greater interest are the criteria offered for determining an adequate insurance fund—namely, as one whose receipts are sufficient to take care of losses and, more crucially, sufficient to generate confidence that even occasional very large losses can be met. As Wallich points out, the international lending field differs from many others in that actuarial calculations of both magnitudes are very uncertain. In this respect, it would seem valuable to estimate levels of insurance which would appear sufficient to achieve the objectives pursued; given the relevance of perceptions and the limited relevance of actuarial calculations in this field, perhaps the simplest way would be through discussions with, or surveys made amongst, bankers.

The need for an outside source of funds is emphasized, although it is defined as temporary (to avoid a subsidy element). This outside source would take care of peak loads in bad years and provide an emergency reserve, but should be paid back over time. An interesting parallel is drawn with the 'pipeline' into the US Treasury established at the inception of the Federal Deposit Insurance Corporation; although *never used*, it gave credibility to US deposit insurance in the early years.

As an illustration of the amounts involved, Wallich assumes US $20 billion of new lending annually, with a 1 per cent annual premium paid and 25 per cent of the liability to be borne by the lender; after five years a total insurance pool of US $3 billion would accumulate, equal to around 13 per cent of the maximum interest loss chargeable to the fund, on the assumption of an interest rate of 10 per cent; alternatively, the insurance fund would have resources of up to 4 per cent in the case of loss of principal. If existing institutions were used, and no special funds allocated for this purpose, 'additionality' becomes a key problem. To what extent would the new private lending generated replace lending that would otherwise have been made by these official institutions, given that the World Bank's charter, for example, reduces its capacity to lend by the same amount as the guarantee? If, however, the guarantee were to cover only a small fraction of the loans (as Wallich suggests), and if such a scheme were effective in promoting significantly larger private flows, the gearing ratio of the funds provided by the official institutions should be far higher than its direct lending; as a result, there would be net additional lending.

Such a scheme would present certain additional advantages to banks, such as reduced taxes for the part of their spread channelled into the insurance pool, and the prospect of liberal supervisory treatment of insured loans. The problems would be the additional cost to the banks, and the fact that insurance would provide rather incomplete protection. Borrowers might benefit from larger flows, if these materialized. They might have to bear part of the cost, and face pressures from the insurer, in addition to those coming from the creditors.

A far more ambitious scheme is the proposal made by Lord Lever[30] to extend the power of the export credit guarantee agencies to insure export of capital (for covering current account deficits) as well as exports of goods. Besides sustaining developing countries' growth and the growth of world trade, such a scheme would contribute to the servicing of trade credits (most of them insured by their export credit insurance agency), thus avoiding defaults or arrears on those credits.

The Lever proposal suggests that export credit agencies set up a central agency, which would fix total and national limits for insured bank lending to LDCs, such limits to be linked to IMF programmes agreed with the borrowing countries. Given that the scheme enhances the role of the IMF, Lever stresses the need that Fund programmes adequately recognize the political and economic problems of LDCs' adjustment. The new lending would come from private banks, but would be insured by national export credit agencies, within the aggregate limit determined by the central insurance agency. This aggregate limit would cover the trading deficit and interest payments on existing debt. Thus, three main features would characterize the new private lending: (i) it would be limited, and related to monitored adjustment programmes; (ii) it would be totally insured by export credit agencies; and (iii) given the quality of the guarantee, it would be long- or medium-term and thus more suitable to the needs of development finance. The scheme does not involve the explicit creation of any new institution, but does imply a significant extension of the role of existing agencies, as well as significantly closer coordination amongst them. The difficulties of achieving such a high degree of coordination are illustrated by the serious problems with the far more limited existing 'consensus' agreements among export credit agencies.

The scheme is estimated by its author to require initially US $40–60 billion of new commercial lending annually for the first year or two, an amount that would be expected to decline over time (this sum seems excessive when total net bank lending to non-oil LDCs in 1984 was expected to reach only around US $20 billion). In any case, the large sums involved would imply, on the one hand, that the scheme could make a significant contribution to the debt problem. On the other hand, there is the drawback that industrial countries' governments would have to agree to give these additional guarantees at a time when existing export credit guarantee schemes are already in financial difficulty. In reply to this type of objection, Lever stresses that, on assumptions far less optimistic than those on which the present policies of industrial governments are based, these government guarantees would not be called upon (and therefore the cost to the taxpayers would be zero); he further argues that, if the debt problem proves more intractable than policy now assumes, the governments' ultimate liability would merely be a substitute for what would otherwise be insupportable further exposure for the banks.

A rather similar proposal to that of Harold Lever has been made by Bolin and Del Canto,[31] with the main focus on providing future credit for LDC imports of capital goods. The proposal is based on a perceived gap in development finance, and on the need for a scheme with strong political appeal, based on support from exporters of capital goods in industrial countries. The fact that it has received favourable evaluation in a recent internal document produced by Business International for the Global One Hundred[32] would indicate that such a scheme is likely to be supported by large industrial multinational companies.

Like the Lever scheme, the proposal suggests an organization backed by the export credit agencies of the main industrial countries. It contemplates an Export Development Fund linked to the World Bank and with access—for a fee—to Bank analyses and loan judgements, as well as its other services, but at the same time legally separate from the Bank, thus allowing it to be more highly leveraged. The new organization would lend within a particular range of maturity, beyond the normal maturities of the World

Bank, funding itself in the floating-rate market. Like the Lever scheme, export credit institutions or some multilateral institution would guarantee repurchase of the notes if necessary; this guarantee would be considered temporary, until a 'track record' was established.

Credits thus granted could involve a package of different maturity loans from different sources, with evaluation by the World Bank and the private banks, and possibly linked by cross-default clauses. Such an extension of an already existing World Bank pilot co-financing scheme could bring important additional advantages for the borrower, in that the loans would not only have a long-term maturity but could also carry a fixed interest rate (with the World Bank temporarily carrying the cost of interest payments if the market rate went above the fixed rate). One of the issues not discussed is the links between the credits granted by the Export Development Fund and those of the national export credit agencies; for example, to what extent would EDF lending be additional to—or a substitute for—existing lending?

Moreover, as Bolin and Del Canto point out, there are a number of issues which need further clarification, several of which refer both to their scheme and to that of Lever. The key questions to be examined are whether national export credit organizations could take a broad cooperative view of their exporters' interests and modify charters or policies to cooperate in a joint effort. Could these organizations promote financing which was not directly and immediately linked (dollar for dollar and mark for mark) to exports from their own countries? At a more institutional level, there are questions about the legal capacity of various export credit organizations to invest in a central institution, or their ability to acquire such authority where it does not exist. (The Lever proposal would seem to imply fewer legal problems, in that credit would still be granted nationally, albeit in an internationally coordinated manner.) There are further issues in relation to the funding of the expanded schemes by the private markets. From the point of view of LDCs, such a scheme would be positive in that it would contribute to fund new investment projects but would not deal with—or even accentuate—the problem, particularly evident in sub-Saharan Africa, but also important in some Latin American economies, of under-utilization of existing capital due to shortages of foreign exchange for financing imports of spare parts and raw materials.

The underlying issue in all these schemes—accentuated in some of the more complex and ambitious proposals outlined below—is that the transnationalization of private financial flows has occurred far faster than the transnationalization of regulatory, supervisory, and other governing rules, as well as government institutions. Many of the proposals being discussed imply steps towards the development of public international institutions corresponding to the rapid development of the private sector. (There is a clear, though not a mechanical, parallel with the development of national central banking long after the development of private national banks.) The issues of the *feasibility* of the proposals are therefore not merely technical, but are closely linked to an understanding of international political and economic forces. In this respect, an understanding of these problems seems to require a combination of analysis by economists and political scientists (the latter with understanding of both national and international relations) and the interaction of such analysts with policy-makers and politicians. Such joint systematic analysis could contribute to a clearer definition of policy proposals that are both technically desirable in an economically and financially interdependent world and politically feasible in a world of independent nation states.

Among the few proposals which explicitly recognize that their implementation would imply a further step in the evolution towards a world central banking structure is that made by George Soros.[33] It is based on a diagnosis which emphasizes two aspects of the LDC debt problem: the negative resource transfer in the short term, and the chronic long-term problem related to the 'debt overhang'. It attempts to reduce the weight of the debt burden, *without* choking off new credits. The explicit objectives are to avert the insolvency of the banking system, to allow the debtor countries to recover, to ensure that the debt burden does not grow faster than the economy which has to support it, and to keep government intervention to a minimum.

The essence of the scheme is interest rate insurance which would cap interest rates above a certain level; the cap could be fixed in absolute terms, or indexed with reference to individual debtor countries' terms of trade. A government agency associated with the central bank would insure lenders in case the cost of their funds rose above the cap. The lenders would pay an insurance premium for this service, and the government agency would use the proceeds to subscribe to the equity capital of a new institution, the International Lending Agency (ILA). The ILA's main role would be to provide the new credit needed to ensure that debtor countries could pay their interest on outstanding loans and still secure economic growth. Thus, the ILA would act as the residual or *balancing supplier of credit* (in this respect there are some parallels with the previous schemes, in particular the Lever one).

The ILA's capital would have two components: premium accounts contributed by the holders of existing loans, and annual contributions by the debtor countries of a certain percentage of their outstanding debt in escrow accounts at the ILA. Furthermore, initially, the ILA's credit would be guaranteed by the industrial countries, for example, through a contingent allocation of SDRs which would be gradually phased out. As a first approximation, the size of the initial guarantees is suggested at around US $40–80 billion. The ILA would establish aggregate country limits. So as not to endow the ILA's management with too much discretionary power, the criteria to determine country limits would be fixed in advance. Interestingly in the context of our perspective, Soros believes that the ILA should not impose an IMF type of adjustment, but should develop its own guide-lines for measuring countries' debt-servicing ability.

The particular feature of the ILA's construction is that, with stable interest rates, the growth of its capital would keep pace with the growth of its liabilities. If interest rates fluctuated excessively, its capital base would be endangered, as its interest equalization account would be overburdened. According to Soros, this should put pressure on the industrial nations in general—and the USA in particular—to prevent excessive interest rate fluctuations. The quality of banks' loan portfolios would also be enhanced, and additional loan loss reserve allocations would become superfluous; insurance premiums would take the place of loan loss reserves (thus providing interest relief rather than being sterilized in the form of reserves). Soros believes that most banks would support such a scheme, as its cost to them would be offset by a decline in the risk of major losses. However, if fluctuations in the interest rate were very large, this risk would by no means be eliminated.

The Soros scheme is one of the most detailed proposals, in that it makes explicit the mechanisms of the operation; it is also very complete, in that it would attempt to tackle a number of the problems raised by debt crises. Partly because of its completeness, however, it is extremely complicated. Furthermore, it does not seem to build enough upon existing institutions, but concentrates on an entirely new institution, the ILA. Although, in abstract terms, new institutions can have important attractions (such as criteria more appropriate to the new problems being faced), in practice they may imply duplication of existing institutions without necessarily leading to major innovations. It is noteworthy also that, since the late 1970s, many new public international institutions have been suggested (for example, the World Development Fund by the Brandt Commission) but none have been created. There are, however, many other interesting ideas in the Soros proposal (such as the contingent use of SDRs for guarantees, or even the concept of a residual or balancing supplier of credit, which is also present, but not so explicitly, in some of the other proposals discussed above) which could be incorporated into schemes more closely linked to existing institutions.

More limited schemes to encourage new flows (as well as to contribute to dealing with the debt overhang) are now under discussion in existing institutions. The International Finance Corporation (IFC) is considering the establishment of investment trusts for individual countries.[34] Trust shares could be issued to new investors, as well as to interested commercial banks, in exchange for some of the banks' existing loans. The trust's manager (probably an investment bank) would then try to exchange the loans for equity stakes in local enterprises. One advantage of this scheme lies in the eventual marketability of investment trust shares, which, with IFC backing, might be attractive to institutions such as pension funds; another advantage would be that the scheme addresses both the immediate financial problems of LDCs caused by their excessive debt and their longer-term problem of insufficient foreign equity capital. Although there may be a need to shift the balance of development finance to non-credit flows, many LDC governments would not welcome large increases in foreign ownership of their assets, particularly if they did not represent new inflows but rather conversion of debt already contracted.

More broadly, the problems created in the past with debt instruments—and particularly their repayment pattern, which is independent of factors affecting the borrowers such as unexpected changes in terms of trade, changes in international interest rates, and the success or otherwise of paticular projects—have focused attention on the greater need for equity-like financial instruments that would link repayments to outcome. In addition to direct foreign investment, other arrangements with this type of feature would include loans indexed to commodity prices or trade levels, non-recourse project loans, and production shares (see also the discussion above on increasing repayment flexibility).

(ii) *Enhancing the stability of the international banking system and of credit flows to LDCs.* One way to achieve these objectives is via an explicit clarification of Central Banks' role as international lenders of last resort (ILLR), accompanied by more stringent and effective supervision.[35] Such schemes emphasize that a large part of international banking activity has been located in the gaps between national regulatory systems, so as to take advantage of asymmetries in the relatively strict banking regulations applying to domestic currencies and residents, and the far looser banking regulations applying to foreign currencies and non-residents. The lack of appropriate explicit ILLR arrangements—parallel to those already established at a national level—is seen to make two undesirable developments more likely. First, there remains the possibility that the widespread financial distress now characterizing the world economy may turn into a major financial crisis; secondly, and more plausibly, the combination of reschedulings and fear of defaults may continue to constrain private bank lending to LDCs.

A proposal made by Griffith-Jones and Lipton,[36] for example, to deal with this set of problems, is for Central Banks of the major industrial countries to make their commitment to ILLR arrangements explicit and formal. This would imply the announcement of a contingency plan, to be activated if a bank were 'in trouble' as a result of its international lending. Such a commitment should contribute to sustain private lending during periods when it would otherwise tend to contract, generally linked to recession and/or financial problems, both national and international. It would be accompanied by far more stringent supervision, which would imply moderating excessive expansion of credit in periods of boom or euphoria; it would also encourage more appropriate forms of lending to LDCs (for example, in relation to maturities). Along similar lines, clear ideas on how supervision could be qualitatively improved have recently been discussed by Lissakers,[37] for example. She suggests that the Cooke Committee should evaluate the possibility of supervising not just individual banks, but the Euro-currency market as a whole, to ensure consistency between the rate of credit creation and stable global economic expansion.

An ILLR scheme, if effective, would contribute indirectly to reducing the pro-cyclical nature of private flows, both at country level and world-wide.[38] It has increasingly been argued that interest rates, terms of trade, and the supply of lending often interact perversely, generating vicious circles of recession and financial distress for individual countries and in the international economy. Hence the growing importance of mechanisms that act as shock-absorbers and play a counter-cyclical role. Just as the CFF directly generates counter-cyclical flows to compensate for fluctuations in export earnings and cost of cereal imports, and an interest rate window and/or interest 'capping' would diminish the impact of fluctuations in interest rates, mechanisms such as an explicit ILLR (accompanied by greater supervision) would reduce fluctuations in private lending. *These three mechanisms combined could make an important, mutually reinforcing contribution to more stable trends, nationally and internationally.* Given that one of the main features of the world economy since the early 1970s has been increased instability in key variables, and that this instability and the resultant uncertainty are seen as negative by different types of economic agents and by different schools of economic thought, measures to enhance prospects for future stability may have a broad base for support.

An important argument against an explicit ILLR declaration is the central banks' repeatedly expressed concern with 'moral hazard', namely the risk that banks will be tempted into imprudent lending if the terms and conditions for ILLR are known in advance. Wallich, the member of the Federal Reserve Board most closely associated with international banking problems, has argued:[39] 'there are dangers in trying to define and publicize specific rules for emergency assistance to troubled banks, notably the possibility of causing undue reliance on such facilities and possible relaxation of needed caution on the part of all market participants.' As a result largely of this perception of 'moral hazard', accompanied by the fear of excessive and uncertain cost of an ILLR, central bankers deliberately do not make explicit ILLR arrangements.

To overcome the problem of 'moral hazard', Griffith-Jones and Lipton have suggested that Bagehot's original concept of 'onerous terms' (good collateral and a punitive rate) could be adapted to present international lending. This could be done by coverting one of the debt-restructuring schemes which has an element of debt discounting (see below) into a contingency plan to be used as an ILLR when particular banks are 'in trouble' as a result of their international lending. The discounted debt would then be re-scheduled at more flexible terms to the debtors. Stringent supervision would provide a second line of defence against 'moral hazard'. The proposal's main aim is to establish a general principle—the need to internationalize the lender of last resort function—but it does not go into details. In particular, it does not attempt the difficult task of estimating the potential cost of such a scheme (like the guarantee scheme, the cost could be zero if explicit defaults and dangers of bank collapses are avoided, but very high if major bank collapses were threatened).

Other schemes have been suggested. An interesting proposal by Johannes Witteveen,[40] former managing director of the IMF, calls for the creation of a facility within the IMF that would insure bank loans against political risks applicable to debtor countries complying with the performance criteria of Fund programmes. Witteveen sees this linked to a major initiative in supervision (via measures such as international reserve requirements under the IMF's control), which would curb excessive credit growth in the future. This proposal would require, as the amount of insured credit grew, an expansion of the Fund's resources, perhaps through guarantees by participating governments. As in several of the other proposals, the key issue would be obtaining support from the major industrial countries for increased guarantees on a considerable scale (without reducing other flows to LDCs), as well as support for significant changes in supervision (the issue of reserve requirements for the Euro-currency market had already been discussed in the 1970s and shelved). Witteveen's proposal would also imply far greater powers for the Fund in regulating international private liquidity, and would increase the role of IMF conditionality for obtaining new credits; the former function— clearly an important measure in the long term—may be unacceptable at present, and would seem to require further study and attention; the latter would clearly be undesirable from the point of view of developing countries, unless and until IMF conditionality were *fundamentally* modified (as discussed above, it seems desirable to us to diminish the already excessive role played by IMF conditionality).

(iii) *Reduction of the 'debt overhang'*. Proposals on this became particularly fashionable at the peak of the debt crisis (mainly in the first half of 1983). As the crisis was seen to have become 'manageable' (at least for the banking system), these proposals were increasingly viewed as contingency plans to be activated only if and when the debt crisis was again perceived as worsening or as not improving sufficiently. This would seem more likely if the international economic environment continued to be unfavourable for a large number of LDCs, and/or if the debtor governments themselves pressed strongly for a reduction in the value of their debt and its servicing. In particular, as discussed above, the continuation in the medium term of high levels of negative net resource transfer from some areas or countries of the third world maintains this as an important option.

To simplify somewhat, most of the proposals have two main features: mechanisms for shifting some or all of the accumulated stock of (non-performing) loans from the books of the banks in return for more marketable and/or less risky assets; and an easing of the debt burden in the short and medium term, through a combination of principal or interest relief or a more limited lengthening of repayments.

One of the relatively more modest proposals is that suggested by Peter Leslie.[41] He stresses that a large proportion of banks' balance sheets will be locked in 'immobilized debt' for a long period, the problem being particularly serious with respect to lending in currencies different from those in which most of the banks' deposits are denominated; for reasons of profitability, capital adequacy, and national prudence, banks may therefore become unwilling to undertake significant new lending, even for normal trade finance. Leslie proposes to mobilize part of the medium-term debt, which has arisen as part of rescheduling, to create fresh lending. The scheme would be linked to export credit, with the corresponding agency or central bank extending its facilities to a bank for discounting a certain amount of a country's debt, provided that the additional cash was then used to make a new export credit to the same country.

In this proposal, the rediscounted debts would come off the balance sheet of the commercial bank, thus no longer requiring appropriate liquidity and prudential capital support; however, they would need to be treated as contingent liabilities, for if the debt was unpaid, a write-off would ultimately have to take place in the books of the commercial bank as the original lender. In this sense, the proposal seems to contain some contradiction; if the debt continues to be the bank's contingent liability, should it not then continue to require prudential capital support? It should be noted, however, that contingent liabilities require less prudential capital support; for example, contingent liabilities are weighted at only half the rate applied to direct liabilities in the Bank of England's own capital system.

More broadly, Leslie's proposal seems to have important similarities with those of Lever and of Bolin and Del Canto; its emphasis on linkage to export credit would make it particularly attractive to those involved in exporting to developing countries, and to those developing countries requiring foreign capital goods (but not to those with already large unused capacity in their existing efficient plants).

A number of far broader proposals for restructuring the debt overhang have been made. We shall describe the main proposals first, and their limitations and advantages at the end of this section.

Perhaps the broadest discounting proposal has come from a US banker, Felix Rohatyn.[42] This was to create a mechanism that would stretch existing bank loans significantly to twenty-five or thirty years, with a low interest rate (ie 6 per cent). A subsidiary of the World Bank or of the IMF, or a totally new institution, guaranteed by the Western governments, would take over the banks' credits in exchange for long-term, low-interest obligations of their own. The banks would clearly suffer loss of current income; Rohatyn does not make it explicit whether they would also have to accept a capital write-off, at the time of swapping their credits for the new instruments, as he implies this to be a matter for further negotiation. Rohatyn's proposal would be on a large scale, as he refers to a sum of around US $300 billion.

A more limited proposal was made by Peter Kenen[43] for the creation of a new international institution, with capital subscribed by industrial countries' governments, which would issue long-term bonds to banks in exchange for LDCs' debts, the latter being exchanged at a discount (for example, of 10 per cent) on their book value. The LDC debts would be rescheduled on a one-time, long-term basis using half of the discount for modest debt relief by either reducing interest rates or granting longer grace periods. A limited period of time would be given for all banks to decide whether to participate, during which period they could exchange only their loans to countries participating in the programme, so as to avoid their selling only their weakest loans. The agency would deal only with debts of those countries which recognized it as successor claimant to the banks, and probably only with those that had an IMF 'seal of approval'.

Weinert's scheme[44] has important similarities with Rohatyn's and Kenen's proposals, but is somewhat more complex. It proposes that the World Bank swaps its bonds for LDC debt held by private banks, the additional capital required for such an operation to be provided through unpaid subscriptions, which according to Weinert would not have immediate budgetary impact. The total value of the banks' assets would not decline, as the bonds would constitute sound assets; the scheme would thus seem not to require a capital write-off. Interest rates on the bonds would be related to countries' capacity to pay the debt for which they were swapped; they would be set annually by the IMF, based on a formula including export volume and terms of trade. They would be below commercial levels, thus implying gradual absorption of losses by banks, but would also carry a minimum rate, to assure banks of the income level required to stay sound; if this minimum exceeded a country's capacity to pay, then the World Bank would pay the necessary difference. This implies another concrete example of how burden-sharing of the debt crises could be implemented in practical terms. Debtor countries' principal repayments would be extended over a long period of time. Banks' participation would be voluntary, and they could choose which LDC debt to swap (though they could not swap all their exposure in a country). Just as Rohatyn's proposal parallels the creation of the Municipal Assistance Corporation—the entity created to revive New York City from bankruptcy—Weinert's proposal follows closely the financial arrangements used by US banks in 1974–5 to reschedule their lending to real estate investment trusts.

Another proposal which, like Weinert's, suggests that repayment is linked to real, measurable capacity to pay, is that made by Norman A. Bailey and his colleagues.[45] According to this scheme, the central banks of the debtor countries would issue equity-like exchange participation notes (EPNs) to their private and official lenders on a pro rata basis to replace the existing amortization schedules; the EPNs would constitute claims on some prudent level of current and future foreign exchange earnings. The notes could be negotiable on the secondary market.

Evaluation of debt-restructuring schemes

The more radical proposals that attempt *de facto* to reduce the total value of LDC debt are based on the correct perception that, unless major changes in the international environment occur, future debt servicing and amortization will continue to be an excessive burden, constraining the growth and development of many LDCs. A large reduction in debt servicing for those countries would clearly make an important contribution to lifting the important foreign exchange constraint on their growth.

A number of problems have been raised, particularly in financial circles, in relation to the more radical proposals. One would be the potential negative impact on banks' capital, reducing their future capacity to lend. This could be dealt with if regulators allowed a gradual write-off of debt, if the new assets which the banks would receive had lower interest but not a lower book value, or if there were a major injection of public funds to compensate banks for their capital write-offs or income reduction. Even if a large proportion of such a public contribution were through a contingent liability and/or spread out through time, the total magnitudes involved clearly make such a contribution unlikely, unless there is a clear threat to the stability of the banks. Furthermore, a large write-off of total LDC debt which was financed to a significant extent by public flows would reduce the availability of new public flows; and, as such a write-off would probably be proportional to existing debt, it would favour those countries able and willing in the past to borrow more, discriminating against countries that could not borrow (particularly low-income ones) and those that followed more cautious development programmes.

Another criticism of the more radical debt-restructuring schemes is that they could help to choke off new lending. It is argued that new lending will be far less likely, since banks will fear that such future debt, like past debt, may also be partly written off, discounted or turned into a low-interest asset; moreover, banks would lose their current incentive to back up their existing debt with new involuntary lending, as has been occurring in the case of many reschedulings to large debtors. An important counter-argument to the latter point is that what matters to LDC governments is the net resource transfer to them, and that, at least in the medium term, debt write-offs would reduce gross borrowing requirements for any given volume of new lending. Furthermore, for most developing countries, the prospects of new loans are very doubtful (see above).

'Moral hazard' is another factor, in that LDCs might seek debt restructuring or relief even when they could have continued to meet orderly payments. Though important, this argument is weakened at a time when about two-thirds of LDC debt is estimated to have been restructured or its payment otherwise delayed, reflecting a general inability of LDCs to repay their debts on schedule.

Finally, many of the debt-restructuring proposals are seen in most international financial circles as too radical and too sweeping, and too sharply opposed to the case-by-case approach adopted so far. Progress may be achieved by studying and defining general guide-lines which would provide a reference framework for individual negotiations in existing fora (for example, Paris Clubs, private debt reschedulings, and consultative groups). Clearly, such guide-lines could not be uniform for all LDCs; they would need to distinguish between countries by level fo income, by the size of their negative net transfers, and by composition of their trade and its price responsiveness, as well as having some flexibility to adapt to the particular conditions of individual countries.

Given that the Paris Club is a long-established rescheduling forum, with total institutional flexibility (it follows no written code of rules), it could clearly provide a useful starting-point for the definition of such guidelines. These could cover longer consolidation periods, or multi-year reschedulings (convenient to both debtors and creditors in cases where there is a large bunching of repayments which clearly cannot be met), as well as minimum grace and repayment periods. The possibility of some subsidy element in the interest rate could be incorporated in this context. Uniform policies for prompt restoration of export credit cover once rescheduling had been agreed would also be important. Such a framework could also be broadened to coordinate the actions of industrial countries as lenders and donors with their role as creditors, which would allow discussions of overall resource transfer flows in a medium-term framework as we have suggested above. Again, this is not a new idea, but builds on procedures already used recently for some countries (the Sudan, for example) and long-established in somewhat different contexts for other countries (for example, aid consortia for India).

Furthermore, a similar attempt could begin to be made to define general guide-lines for private debt reschedulings, referring to aspects similar to those just mentioned for the Paris Club. Some of the schemes discussed—such as interest capping, either in its liquidity or its concessional version—could be relatively easily introduced within such a framework. Some of the broader proposals, linking debt restructuring to new flows, could also be accommodated within a revised and broader framework of existing procedures for bank debt rescheduling.

To conclude, we would like first to agree with the Commonwealth Secretariat *Report on the Debt Crisis* that 'any workable set of arrangements is likely to be *eclectic* in character, combining several of the more attractive features of the prototype schemes, by dealing simultaneously with the debt overhang, new lending and strengthening the banking system against the possibility of major shocks'.

Abstract discussions on what exact mix of changes would be optimal have already been going on for a couple of years. We believe that the time has come for general discussions to be transformed into policy actions, and that this transformation will only occur as a result of sufficient pressure from the debtors themselves; it seems increasingly inevitable that, for such debtor pressure to be effective, it must contain some element of unilateral action!

Notes

1. For a clear statement from a Latin American perspective, see R. Devlin, 'The Burden of the Debt and the Crisis: Should a Unilateral Solution be Reached?', *ECLA Review* 22, 1984. For a Commonwealth perspective, see Commonwealth Secretariat, *The Debt Crisis and the World Economy*, report by a Commonwealth group of experts, London, 1984. For a statement based on a theoretical model, see P. Krugman, 'International Debt Strategies in an Uncertain World', in G. Smith and J. Coddington, eds., *International Debt and the Developing Countries*, Washington, DC, 1985.

2. A. Kaletsky, *The Cost of Default*, New York, 1985.

3. Krugman, 'International Debt Strategies in an Uncertain World'.

4. As the 1984 Inter-American Development Bank's *1984 Economic and Social Progress* report shows, the generation of large trade surpluses in Latin America (required to fund the negative net transfers of financial resources) has basically been reflected until now in a large decline in the region's rate of investment, which fell by 6 per cent of the region's GNP between 1981 and 1983.

5. F. Castro, 'How and Why the Unpayable Foreign Debt of Latin America and the Third World Must be Cancelled and the Urgent Need for a New International Economic Order', interview given to the Mexican newspaper *Excelsior*, 21 March 1985 (reproduced in English in *Gramma Weekly Review*, 7 April 1985).

6. O. Sunkel, *America Latina y la Crisis Economica Internacional: Ocho Tesis y una Propuesta*, Buenos Aires, 1975.

7. *Financial Times*, 21 September 1985, 'IADB Urges Fund to Aid Latin American Debtors'.

8. Kaletsky, *The Cost of Default*.

9. To some extent banks have already begun to exert such pressure: see, for example, for an important statement, 'Institute of International Finance Calls on Fund to Provide More Financing to Debtor Nations', *IMF Survey*, 15 April 1985. Such demands would become far stronger and more concrete in the case of a conciliatory moratorium.

10. Business Latin America, 'US Policy in Latin America: The Second Term of the Reagan Administration', 6 March 1985.

11. For a similar proposal, see for example the *Literature Survey* (mimeo, Brighton, 1984), prepared for the Independent Consultants' Study of Aid Effectiveness, prepared for the Task Force on Concessional Flows', set up by the IMF Development Committee (Study published as R. H. Cassen and Associates, *Does Aid Work?*, Oxford, 1986).

12. See, for example, R. Green and S. Griffith-Jones, *Third World Affairs* (issued annually), 1986 issue, London.

13. R. Dornbusch, 'The Debt Problems and Options for Debt Relief', mimeo, Cambridge, Mass., 1984.
14. See J. Williamson, *A New SDR Allocation?*, Washington, DC, March 1984.
15. L. M. Goreux, *Compensatory Financing Facility*, pamphlet series 34, Washington, DC, 1980
16. See, for example, S. Griffith-Jones, *Compensatory Financing Facility: A Review of its Operations and Proposals for Improvement*, report to the Group of Twenty-Four, UNDP/UNCTAD, Project INT/81/046, January 1983.
17. See Mexican Government, 'Facility to Finance the Balance of Payments Deficit Caused by the Rise in Interest Rate', *The Economist*, 2 April 1983, and Cline, *International Debt, Systemic Risk and Policy Response*.
18. Calculations based on data in World Bank, *World Debt Tables 1983–84, First Supplement*, Washington, DC, April 1984.
19. Anthony Solomon, president of the Federal Reserve Bank of New York, proposed an interest cap (*Journal of Commerce*, 10 May 1984). Henry Wallich, Governnor of the Federal Reserve Board, broached a wider proposal for interest capping, such that any interest in excess of inflation plus a normal real interest rate would be capitalized: H. Wallich, 'The Problems of the World Banking Community—A Central Banker's View', remarks at the *Financial Times* World Banking Conference, December 1983.
20. As has been discussed, for example, in American Express Bank, 'International Debt: Banks and the LDCs', *AMEX Bank Review*, Special Paper 10, March 1984.
21. Estimates based on information in W. Cline, *International Debt and the Stability of the World Economy*, Washington, DC, September 1983.
22. D. R. Lessard, *North–South Finance: The Implications of Overreliance on Bank Credit*, Working Paper, Cambridge, Mass., MIT, Sloan School of Management, August 1984.
23. C. Massad and R. Zahler, 'The Process of Adjustment in the Eighties: The Need for a Global Approach', *ECLA Review* 23, August 1984.
24. For a discussion of 'bisque clauses' in the context of developing countries' external finance, see C. Harvey, 'On Reducing the Risk in Foreign Finance—for Both Parties?', IDS Discussion Paper, 1981.
25. N. Bailey, 'A Safety Net for Foreign Lending', *Business Week* 10, January 1983.
26. See, for example, UNCTAD, *Review of Implementation of Guidelines Approved in Resolution 22 XXI Related to Developing Countries' Debt Problems*, New York, January 1984.

27. S. Griffith-Jones, *The Paris Club and the Poorer Countries*, background document for the Study of Aid Effectiveness (see note 11 above), commissioned by the Development Committee, mimeo, Brighton, June 1984.

28. W. H. Bolin and J. Del Canto, 'LDC Debt: Beyond Crisis Management', *Foreign Affairs*, summer 1983.

29. H. Wallich, 'Insurance of Bank Lending to Developing Countries', New York, 1984.

30. H. Lever, 'The International Debt Threat: A Concerted Way Out', *The Economist*, 9 July 1983.

31. Bolin and Del Canto, 'LDC Debt'.

32. Business International, *Debt and Development: Searching for New Vistas*, mimeo, New York, 1984.

33. G. Soros, *International Debt Reform*, mimeo New York, 1984.

34. The account is based on C. Gwyn, 'The IMF and the World Bank: Measures to Improve the System', in R. Feinberg and V. Kallab, eds., *Uncertain Future: Commercial Banks and the Third World*, Washington, DC, 1984.

35. See D. R. Lessard, 'Appropriate Non-concessional Industrial Financing for Developing Countries', paper prepared for UNIDO/PC.48, London, 20 July 1982.

36. See S. Griffith-Jones and M. Lipton, 'International Lenders of Last Resort: Are Changes Required?', Midland Bank Occasional Paper in International Trade and Finance, London, 1984; also J. Guttentag and R. Herring, 'The Lender-of-Last-Resort Function, in an International Context', Essay in International Finance 151, Princeton, NJ, May 1983; and G. G. Johnson with R. K. Abrams, 'Aspects of the International Safety Net', IMF Occasional Paper 17, Washington, DC, 1983.

37. K. Lissakers, 'Bank Regulation and International Debt', in Feinberg and Kallab, eds., *Uncertain Future*.

38. In this sense, the ILLR would have close parallels with the classical concept of *national* lender of last resort—clarified by Bagehot—as an institution which accepts the obligation to maintain liquidity of financial intermediaries in a crisis; this is different from counter-cyclical lending to *borrowers*, e.g. by the IMF, which has, perhaps somewhat loosely, also been called international lending of last resort.

39. H. Wallich, 'Central Banks as Regulators and Lenders of Last Resort in an International Context: A View from the United States', *Key Issues in International Banking*, Federal Reserve Bank of Boston Conference Series 18, October 1977. Also, personal communication, June 1983.

40. J. Witteveen, 'Developing a New International Monetary System: A

Long Term View', 1983 Per Jacobsson Lecture, summarized in *IMF Survey*, 10 October 1983.

41. P. Leslie, 'Techniques of Rescheduling: The Latest Lessons', *The Banker*, April 1983. Also based on interview with Peter Leslie.

42. F. Rohatyn, 'A Plan for Stretching out Global Debt', *Business Week*, 28 February 1983; and 'New Bretton Woods Conference Needed', *Financial Times*, World Banking Supplement, 9 May 1983. Rohatyn is chairman of the Municipal Assistance Corporation of New York, and partner in the investment banking firm of Lazard Freres.

43. P. Kenen, 'Dealing with Third World Debt', *New York Times*, 6 March 1983.

44. R. S. Weinert, 'Banks and Bankruptcy', *Foreign Policy*, spring 1983.

45. Bailey, 'A Safety Net for Foreign Lending'.

CHAPTER II

Towards Reactivation and New Development Strategies

We have argued in this book that the so-called debt crisis is no mere financial phenomenon. Instead, it is the most visible and dramatic international financial manifestation of a very deep-seated crisis which marks the end of the development boom of the post-war era.

This broader crisis has many aspects, of which we have chosen to concentrate on the following: the profound and prolonged recession that has affected Latin America since 1982 (Chapters 2 and 8); the development crisis that was affecting the Latin American economies already at the end of the 1960s (Chapter 2), which could be ignored thanks to the financial permissiveness of the 1970s (Chapter 6); the collapse of the public international financial system created in Bretton Woods (Chapters 4, 5, and 6); and the increasing instability and decline in the long-term rate of growth of the industrial economies during the 1970s, and most probably for some time to come (Chapters 7 and 9).

Given the poor prospects of the leading industrial economies for the foreseeable future, and the international financial and debt crisis, we have devoted Chapter 10 to a review of proposals and our own suggestions concerning the need for a new system of international financial intermediation. Given the boom in literature on this subject, stimulated by the debt crisis and its increasing unmanageability, and the great number and variety of proposals, this is one of the longest chapters of the book.

The present chapter, concerned with new development strategies for Latin America, will on the contrary be somewhat more brief. This is not because the subject does not require an extensive and profound treatment, but because there is so little to dwell upon in the present discussion.

The present recession has been treated as just any other recession, with the hope that it will evaporate in a short time, and that growth will be resumed soon. Moreover, the emphasis has been on the debt problem as a financial matter, rather than on the background of more profound national and international development problems discussed earlier. Furthermore, the urgency and immediacy of the financial and foreign exchange *débâcle* has concentrated the attention of governments almost exclusively on fiscal, monetary, and balance of payments matters. These matters are entirely in the hands of financial authorities, mainly central banks and ministries of finance, and the discussion has been restricted to 'crisis management' (Chapter 8).

At another level, the whole subject of long-term development policies, strategies, and planning has been more or less abandoned in the last decade, after enjoying a prolonged boom in the 1960s. Development has become an important subject for political scientists, sociologists, and other social scientists, but it has lost almost all interest as far as the discipline of economics is concerned. There are at least two explanations for this.

As has already been suggested in Chapter 6, the growing integration and transnationalization of national economies during the 1960s and 1970s, and particularly the process of financial transnationalization, led to a change in the power structure. This became dominated by sectors related to international and internal trade and finance, with the corresponding strengthening of the ideology of free trade and liberal neoclassical market economics and monetarism, all of it supported politically by the advent of the radically conservative governments of Thatcher and Reagan in the late 1970s.

On the other hand, although substantial economic growth, industrialization, and modernization was achieved in many of the developing countries through import substitution strategies, the development process showed serious flaws in many respects, particularly as regards external disequilibria and the inability of the process to solve the problems of poverty, unemployment, and equity. Most of the economic profession turned to neoclassical and neoliberal approaches as a source of critique, and as an alternative developmental paradigm.

To explain the failures of development strategies, those more concerned with development than with conventional economics and economic growth turned to, or re-emphasized, factors such as income distribution and poverty, social attitudes and values, institutions, population dynamics, resource endowments and their appropriation, science and technology, the nature of international relations, and international as well as national power structures. But these kinds of *variables* of development are precisely those which economics, and particularly neoclassical and monetarist economics, consider *constants*. One has to turn back, and then, it is hoped, move ahead, to political economy, to find those kinds of longer-term, structural variables integrated into an analysis of development. Conventional economics, being concerned almost exclusively with short-term flows of income and expenditure and their balance in various markets, has become unable to deal with the other, far more significant questions of development enumerated above.

It also has difficulty in perceiving that behind the debt problem and the recession, which are seen as short-term, financial disequilibria, there looms a profound development crisis of a structural and long-term nature, as we have attempted to show in this book. Questions of short-term equilibrium, optimum efficiency in the allocation of resources, and the smooth functioning of markets become particularly relevant when growth is assured or can be taken for granted, but the achievement of those conditions are not sufficient for generating growth. This is the basic fallacy of the so-called 'adjustment' programmes, in the case of dependent underdeveloped economies, in an international environment characterized by slow and unstable growth in the industrial economies, and where private international capital flows and the international private capital market have turned perverse, extracting rather than contributing to domestic savings and investment.

Under these conditions, high capital accumulation, a central condition for growth and for the possibility of development, has become completely impossible. The service of the debt means not only that a substantial trade surplus has to be achieved, but also that a substantial proportion of domestic savings has to be transferred abroad. This has generated the transfer problem, the conversion of internal savings into hard currency, a problem that has created the concern with the questions of international finance and trade that prevails in the literature on the debt problem. But there is the other problem, of how to generate the domestic savings necessary to generate the trade surplus.[1] This problem has at least three crucial aspects.

Domestic savings used to be complemented to a substantial

degree by foreign savings (and by the corresponding *deficit* in current account) to achieve the investment level which allowed these countries considerable growth. To maintain that level of investment, in current circumstances domestic savings would have to increase not only to a level similar to that of investment, but substantially above it, since such savings would have to finance the additional savings necessary to compensate for the debt service. This would imply an increase in the average domestic savings rate from substantially below to well above the investment rate, which means an increase in the marginal savings rate that is so high that it seems quite impossible to achieve in the short or even the medium term.

The second aspect is that the considerable savings effort which these countries would have to make to service their foreign debt is difficult to reconcile with a recessionary adjustment policy, which reduces personal incomes, business profits, and government revenues, and therefore the sources of savings.

The third consideration, which is the one that has been voiced most forcefully and with increasing urgency, especially by the political leaders of the Latin American countries, is the sociopolitical contradiction. The situation of stagnant levels of economic activity, substantially under-utilized capacity, with high rates of unemployment and underemployment, decreasing real wages, declining social expenditures and services, and increasing poverty, is becoming unacceptable to the increasing number of democratic regimes in Latin America.

The main responsibility of the new Latin American governments elected in recent years is to their own peoples, and not to transnational banks. Their legitimacy, even if obtained through democratic elections, may be challenged if they are perceived as sacrificing their people, without any hope of being rewarded in the near future, in order to maintain the profits of the seven or eight largest US banks which are responsible for a large proportion of Latin America's foreign debt. This relates particularly to that part of the debt used for rather dubious purposes, which have scarcely benefited the majority of the people.

Social and political tension could reach such levels in this case that governments will either have to change their policies, suspending foreign debt service totally or at least partially, and giving priority to expanded internal production, employment and income—whatever the consequences—or be swept away by popular pressure. They would be replaced either by another government that would respond to popular demands, or by governments that would suppress them through a renewed wave of repression.

Democratic governments cannot but try to avoid this outcome, and they will increasingly feel completely justified in doing so, particularly since they have followed recessionary adjustment policies for several years and have made strenuous efforts to service their debts. If the developed countries' governments do not respond with policies that help the debtor countries to grow and service the debts, they will be responsible—together with the banks who lent excessively in the first place—if the debtor countries refuse to continue to play a game that punishes them so severely.

In 1935, Gustavo Ross, the Chilean finance minister, negotiated an agreement with the creditors by which the service of the debt was changed from a fixed rate to a proportion of the profits of the nitrate and copper industries. He justified it very simply: 'a respectable country must make an effort to honour its financial commitments. The service of our obligations must be made on a real and simple basis. We are the owners of the main known wealth of natural nitrate and we exploit large copper resources. If they buy from us nitrate and copper in sufficient quantities and at reasonable prices, we will be able to pay; if not, they will be responsible for our poverty and they will have no right to complain.'[2] The same linkages between debt service and trade growth are present today.

The economic and sociopolitical contradictions of present short-term adjustment policies urgently require a renewed discussion of policies of recovery and development. The development policies of Latin America since the Second World War have been inspired by two main theoretical sources: post-Keynesian developmentism and neoliberal monetarism. Obviously, reality is always more complex and finely shaded than analytical distinctions, but the latter fulfill a useful function of conceptual clarification. The purpose here is to single out two theoretical conceptions that inspire different policies, and two historical periods, in which first one prevails and then the other, until they culminate in the current crisis, when once again they dispute the leading role.

Post-Keynesian developmentism places emphasis on internal affairs, on the development of the material productive forces of industry, of agriculture, of the basic social capital and human resources infrastructure; externally, on Latin American integration and public international cooperation. The state and planning play a major role in the promotion of social and economic development, and in international relations. This approach prevailed during the 1950s and 1960s, with varying degrees of intensity and coherence in different countries.

Neoliberal monetarism—with its emphasis on the liberalization of the money, goods, services, and labour markets, on external openness in respect of trade and finance, and on the development of private internal financial systems, and its promotion of private and market economic agents in preference to the state and to planning—began to establish itself in the 1960s and prevailed in many countries in the 1970s.

This transition—in some cases moderate, pragmatic, complex, and intelligent, but not so much in others—reached extremes of ideological radicalization in a number of instances, particularly in the countries of the Southern Cone. Although these national differences were determined, to a great extent, by the historical experience and the economic, social, and political structures of each country, the general trend towards a transition from development strategies that were more protectionist and state-controlled to others more open to international forces and to private business was undoubtedly connected with the changing international trends of the post-war decades.

The great world depression of 1929–32 and the Second World War initially encouraged Keynesian development strategies. In contrast, the process of expansion of the international private financial system and the post-war growth of trade accentuated the influence of neoclassical economics. The present deep crisis now confronts practically every country with a crucial economic policy dilemma: either submission to an extremely severe recessive adjustment of a monetarist character, such as transnational financial capitalism is trying to impose, or recovery, and maintenance, of a sufficient degree of freedom to implement reactivating policies in the framework of a strategy based on the development of national and regional productive and social forces.

To serve the debt or not to serve it, that is the question today.

All the Latin American governments declare that they want to serve it in the long term; but many have been unable to do so, and have left matters in suspense for spells of several months. Nor have they been able to let this situation drag on for any greater length of time, finding themselves in most cases compelled to negotiate an agreement with the IMF. This latter is imposing monetarist policies of severe restriction of demand, designed to generate trade surpluses, in exchange for which it facilitates the refinancing of the debt with small contributions of its own funds and from the creditor banks. These agreements have managed to survive in some cases, but in others have been unable to withstand internal sociopolitical pressures, so that this very short-term cycle starts all over again. Thus the Latin American and other developing economies have gone on for several years, waiting for Godot to bring a world reactivation and growth that has not yet come and will probably not reappear for a long time.

This reveals a situation in which the costs of serving the debt and of not serving it are both intolerable in terms of economic and social cost and of political instability. The transnational banks and the developed countries are prepared to accept temporary moratoria, and prefer short-term refinancing, a sign that they fear the consequences of a financial breakdown; but they do not dare to embark upon substantial long-term refinancing or financing, a sign that they place no reliance on the resumption of dynamic international development or on the payment capacity of the debtor countries.

It is essential to avoid catastrophic options, as well as the current deterioration. To that end, an international and national strategy of greater scope and breadth would need to be designed. It would be a question of establishing common basic principles for the creation of a new set of international public institutions to support development and the dynamization and stability of the international economy. Within this framework, each country would be able to choose to renegotiate its debt or not, according to its own special circumstances, but in a context that favoured development rather than hampering it. However, the suggestions in this direction that have been made year after year have met with little response in the leading industrialized countries, although the recent initiatives by US Finance Secretary Baker are steps—albeit small ones—in the right direction.

Furthermore, it is absolutely essential that the industrial countries should start out again on the road of economic expansion, and should reopen their economies to international trade on the basis of active industrial and agricultural readjustment policies and the maintenance of policies of full utilization of production capacity. The BIS itself recognizes that room for manœuvre has been created which makes greater economic activity possible without the risk of unmanageable inflationary pressures, and that restrictive monetarist policies have been carried too far. Nevertheless, the analysis presented in the foregoing chapters reveals the serious structural and political obstacles to such an advance.

The exorbitant external debt accumulated by most of the Latin American countries is the responsibility of the transnational banks, of the governments of the industrial countries, and of the governments and ruling classes of the debtor countries. The servicing of this debt is impossible on a basis of reducing the debtor economies to a state of stagnation, which will probably lead to default. It is therefore indispensable that the cost of debt servicing should be shared by those responsible for the debt and those that have enjoyed its ephemeral benefits. At the international level, the transnational banks and the governments of the industrial countries must assume their quota of responsibility, facilitating debt servicing. In addition, these countries must provide new long-term credit at low rates of interest, so that reactivation can be achieved through new development strategies in the debtor economies.

At the internal level, the more heavily indebted the Latin American countries are, the more need they have to reformulate their development policies, directing them towards four fundamental objectives: concentration of available resources on meeting the basic needs of the majorities, employment, selective export expansion and diversification, and import substitution. Only a reasonable and sustainable proportion of the foreign exchange obtained from export earnings should be allocated to debt servicing: the rest should be reserved for importing essential goods directly or indirectly for popular consumption and capital accumulation, the latter in its turn to be used exclusively to satisfy popular consumer requirements, selected export activities, and accumulation itself. The restriction of non-essential consumer imports and production would be the contribution of the privileged sectors of debtor countries to the servicing of the external debt for which they were partly responsible.

The adoption of measures favouring an internal reactivation geared to the application of a new development strategy calls for a freedom of manœuvre in economic policy which current agreements with the IMF prevent. As was pointed out, the crucial dilemma facing economic policy at the present time is the question of how to achieve a severe compression of imports which will allow a considerable trade surplus to be built up for the purpose of serving the external debt. The monetarist prescription, one of the main objectives of which is to maintain or obtain external openness, consists in restricting global expenditure on consumption and investment to the point at which demand for imports dwindles sufficiently for this objective to be attained, while it is assumed at the same time that in this way resources will be set free to increase exports.

According to our analysis, and that of many others, this approach is mistaken and over-burdensome in economic and social terms. It is mistaken, because the mobility of the factors of production is low, particularly in a context of low investment rates. A rapid and considerable expansion of the value of exports is very unlikely, particularly while deliberate medium-term policies at the national and international level are not followed. It is over-costly, in terms of employment and popular consumption, because it is socially more efficient for the import function to be modified by direct acts of selective intervention, to restrict imports through taxes, tariff duties, and import and exchange controls, discriminating between those that are essential and those that are less critical. This ensures a level of investment, production, and essential consumption which will minimize the effect of the crises on employment and the standard of living of the lower-income sectors. While this policy involves a change in relative prices and assuredly a rise in price levels, it does not (and should not) imply uncontrollable inflation, in so far as idle capacity exists, a tax policy is applied which strictly limits the income and expenditure of the more affluent sectors, and an incomes policy is adopted which prevents unjustified wage increases.

Economic policy also requires enough freedom of manœuvre for short-term reactivating measures to form part of a long-term development strategy, oriented towards the objectives indicated above, and founded primarily on those natural, human, and infrastructure resources with which most of these countries are fairly comfortably endowed, and which constitute the only sound and permanent basis for sustained development.

Obviously, the less the negative international context improves and the less support is given to reform proposals in respect of trade, finance, and investment, the more austere these policies will have to be. It is urgently necessary to face up to the possibility that perhaps nothing of any significance may be obtained by developing countries' governments from the industrialized world or the international institutions, and carefully to explore what this would mean in terms of development strategies designed to cope with such a situation.

The lessons taught by history must be learnt. A development of the productive forces which is directly channelled towards the satisfaction of the basic needs of the majorities and the elimination of dependence cannot be achieved through the massive incorporation of a transnational development style of the individualist–consumist type, making highly intensive use of imported capital, energy, and technology. This has not been possible either through the deliberate promotion of such 'modernization' (post-Keynesian developmentism) or—much less still—though indiscriminate external openness and privatization (monetarism), even in an exceptionally favourable international context. The transnational style simply cannot be generalized to the whole of Latin American society. In the best instance, the case of developmentism, it benefits a more or less sizeable minority, according to the country concerned; but large sections of the population linger on in hopeless poverty. In the case of monetarism, economic, social, and political concentration and polarization is far greater, development and diversification of the structure of production far smaller, and external vulnerability and dependence are overwhelming.

It cannot but be recognized that true national and regional development will have to be based mainly on transformation of the resources and natural environment in which Latin America is relatively rich, incorporating the efforts of the entire population, together with the adoption of life-styles and consumption patterns, techniques, and modes of organization appropriate to this natural and human environment; with very prudent and efficient utilization of the little capital available, especially its imported component; and all this with the explicit aim of producing goods and services and accumulating the basic social capital required by the majority sectors of the population, to improve their levels of living and of productivity. It must not be forgotten that in this respect Latin America has substantially improved its potential in recent decades. If many countries could move ahead dynamically in the 1930s, under much more difficult international conditions and with substantially inferior internal capabilities, they should be much more capable of doing so now.

Regional cooperation must play a role of the greatest importance in these new internal and international tasks. This means, at the level of North–South negotiations, persisting in the promotion of a reform of the international system along the lines suggested above and, in this context, supporting the renegotiation of the external debt of countries compatible with growth, but at the same time exploring the alternatives that might be adopted should this line of action fail. A second aspect of supreme significance is the revitalization of the regional integration institutions, which will facilitate inter-Latin American trade, payments, and investment. A further crucial aspect is support for all possible forms of integration and cooperation as between the Latin American region and the rest of the third world. Lastly, it would be impossible to exaggerate the importance of economic and technical cooperation, in every respect, and particularly as regards exchange of experience and information on all topics pertinent to the new national and international development strategies suggested.

From the type of analysis set forth, it is obvious that the proposals put forward, both at the domestic and at the international and regional level, imply radical political changes. In the last analysis, it is necessary that the predominance of international trade and financial interests and their respective local transnational bases be replaced by broad national coalitions, representative of a majority of social sectors, which accord priority to the reduction of poverty, expansion of employment and economic activity, and more progressive income distribution.

This happened in many countries after the 1930s crisis, and it may be that the crisis of today will do much to enforce a similar change. But this is not a matter of history repeating itself. There are now new social sectors which did not exist in the past, or which were ousted or bypassed by recent development policies. They include, among others, the vast marginal urban sectors and the vast rural sectors of extreme poverty, the new contingents of young people who have had access to education, the labour force resulting from the incorporation of women into the labour market, the important, highly skilled middle strata, all of which would have to be well represented in the formulation and implementation of the new development strategy that is needed now to overcome the crisis. This is perhaps the most important of the many issues that will have to be very seriously tackled as part of the effort to find new paths to development.

It is of course not possible to recommend one single strategy for all or even most Latin American countries. This presumption of universality has probably been one of the most serious sins of both main strategies followed in the past, and particularly of the more recent, neoliberal variety. The post-Keynesian import-substitution strategy was at least based on a diagnosis of some of the fundamental structural characteristics common to most of the Latin American economies, even though it did not differentiate sufficiently amongst them. Neoliberalism has ignored *both* the common *and* the particular characteristics of those economies.

This is perhaps one of the main reasons why import-substitution strategies, while generating serious imbalances of various kinds, managed at least to engineer economic growth and modernization, undoubtedly creating improved conditions for further development. By contrast, neoliberalism, at least where it was carried to extremes, as in the countries of the Southern Cone, did not achieve growth, often led to de-industrialization, and aggravated the problems of inequality, unemployment, and external disequilibria. This sin of universality in development strategies has been elevated to new heights by IMF-sponsored adjustment programmes, except in a few countries which have had the political and technical capacities to adopt their own adjustment policies or negotiate varieties of the IMF formulae.

New development strategies ought to be based on a new pragmatism, based on a critical appraisal of past failures and achievements of both main strategies followed so far, on a realistic appraisal of the new international conditions prevailing in the present, and probably for the next several years, and should be specially concerned with the particular conditions and problems of each country.

As regards this latter aspect, not only ought conditions relating to the current short-term situation be taken into account—such as inflation rates, the debt situation, fiscal, monetary, and balance of payments conditions—but also factors relating to long-term development.

In order for these policies to lead to new development strategies, it is also of fundamental importance that structural factors of development are also taken into account, such as size and location of the country, resource endowments and population dynamics, degree of industrialization and of urbanization, social and political structure, and role of the state. The Central American and Caribbean economies can obviously not follow strategies similar to those of the larger and more industrialized economies of the region, Mexico's proximity to the USA is a crucial factor for that society. Moreover, to emerge from a decade of extreme neoliberal development strategies is not the same as having had a more moderate experience in this respect.

All of this is another strong reason for avoiding the previously prevailing arrogance with respect to development strategies, and for limiting our concluding remarks to some reminders of some very fundamental lessons learnt from past developments and the present situation, in the hope that they will contribute to a renewed discussion of development issues at both international and national levels, where, after all, the final decisions will have to be taken.

The present economic crisis has been compared, in terms of depth and extension, with the Great Depression of 1929–32. However, there is a fundamental difference between the two. The present crisis is taking place in far more modern and urban societies; societies whose population and whose economic and sociopolitical activities are highly concentrated in metropolitan areas. In view of this, the acute tensions and conflicts which have characterized the Latin American scene in recent years should come as no surprise.

In spite of the terrifying economic and social toll which the crisis is taking in almost all Latin American countries, no full awareness of the dramatic current situation seems yet to have developed. We still seem to be under the sway of a sort of mental inertia, arising from the exceptional period of economic growth which took place in the 1950s and 1960s and the financial boom of the 1970s. There is still confidence that the crisis will soon be overcome, and that we shall return to the 'normal state of affairs' of past decades. But reality in no way justifies these expectations. The projection in the conditions for long-term growth in the central economies and the international economy are far less favourable for the future than those which existed in the post-war decades. In particular, prospects for terms of trade, investment, and finance are discouraging. On top of all this, we have to add the enormous and ever-growing weight of the external debt, whose servicing seriously constrains the chances of even minimal growth in our economies.

It follows from this that, as previously suggested, in the future we shall be faced with a situation marked by a lower level of world economic growth than in the past, and a minimum level of external financing, which will make it difficult to ensure supplies of the minimal requirements of the poorer section of the population, and to assure future growth.

In consequence, we shall have no choice but to face up to the structural crisis in our development which was already latent towards 1970, but which we were able to postpone thanks to the peculiar financial circumstances which prevailed during the 1970s. This is the essential reason—leaving aside the serious social injustice and the acute political tensions they involve—why short-term adjustment policies have no future. They assume that, once the adjustment has been made, we shall return to a fairly normal situation. This is not so, however. The successive adjustments, particularly in the new international circumstances, will not lead us back to normal, but towards an encounter with a deep and longstanding structural crisis, significantly worsened by policies which for a decade and a half have sought to avóid it, and rendered even more acute by the present recessionary policies.

In view of the traumatic experiences of the recent past and the sombre prospects for the immediate future, the central theme which preoccupies Latin American countries at this critical moment in their history is the need to overcome as soon as possible the cost of a recessionary adjustment through an expansionary adjustment. Such an expansionary adjustment would also constitute the basis for a transition towards a form of development which will provide a strong support for democracy, as well as being sustainable in the medium and long term. In order to approach these questions in a positive way it is necessary to distinguish between short-term *flows* and the substantial *endowments* of population, natural resources, and productive assets which have been acquired and built up over the longer term. Taking a broader view of the three classical factors of production —labour, land, and capital—we must recognize that the productive capabilities and sociopolitical and administrative abilities of Latin American countries have reached fairly advanced levels in many cases, and cannot and will not be left idle for much more time as a consequence of the external squeeze. The situation must be approached from a political economy point of view, which offers the advantage of being able to establish links between the accumulated sociocultural and the political capabilities, as well as with the spatial, natural resource, and environmental potentialities, and with that of the accumulated productive capacity. This viewpoint also constitutes a bridge to connect medium- and long-term development with annual flows and short-term policies. These latter are principally concerned with macroeconomic equilibria: fiscal, monetary, external, employment, and income indicators, and their sociopolitical implications and constraints. In the present crisis, the serious external disequilibrium in the short-term flows of income and expenditure requires a considerable restriction of imports, but leads to a pronounced under-utilization of the potential of the accumulated sociocultural, natural, and productive heritage. This means that we are in the presence of a considerable potential in terms of real resources which may be mobilized, to the extent that such mobilization can free itself from its dependence on imported inputs.

This approach also helps to clarify the problem posed by the passage from a recessionary adjustment to an expansionary one, and the transition to development. The recessionary adjustment essentially involves manipulation of the short-term tools of economic policy, whose purpose is to restrict overall demand, cutting public expenditure, reducing investment, bringing down wages and salaries, limiting expansion of the money supply, and devaluing the currency, with the common purpose of reducing imports, but with serious consequences for accumulation, production, wages, employment, and the use of the accumulated social assets. Instead of simply concentrating on containing demand and imports, an expansionary readjustment will have to combine a selectively restrictive policy towards demand with a selectively expansionary policy towards supply, making use initially of idle productive capacity. This involves changing the make-up of both demand and supply, with the aim of achieving a reciprocal adjustment.

The first step would be to try to make some use of this sociocultural, natural, and productive potential and available idle capital; and the second step—a medium- and long-term one—would involve investment, institutional, and sociocultural policies aimed at modifying the nature of this social, natural, and capital stock. Whereas recessionary demand policies rely on the market to impose its own selectivity, with all too well-known regressive effects on income and wealth, given the structure of income and power, a combined policy of selective restriction of demand and selective expansion of supply, focused on dynamic poles of growth, would need to make efficient use of state planning and intervention. This raises the question of the state, its effectiveness and representativity, but also offers the opportunity for democratic political dialogue, in so far as the costs and benefit of such selectiveness are fairly shared out.

There exists a whole wealth of knowledge, experience, and proposals of a macroeconomic and sociopolitical nature, together with more detailed knowledge of a sectoral nature and specific programmes, which can serve to formulate concrete proposals for an expansionary readjustment, with its whole accompanying range of selective measures and programmes. Many of such measures are in fact already being implemented as a reaction to the crisis. These involve programmes, aimed at large, medium, and small enterprises and at informal activities, whose purpose is to lighten the burden of poverty, provide employment, satisfy basic needs, produce exports, and replace imports.

Amongst such measures, it is worth mentioning programmes involving massive use of labour for the construction and recon- struction of housing, drainage works, infrastructure, and collective service equipment in areas of popular settlement; for the construc- tion, reconstruction, and maintenance of the highway network, public works, and human settlements in general; protection against flooding and other natural catastrophes; reafforestation, the building of terraces in areas of erosion, cleaning and protecting rivers and canals; drainage and irrigation works; opening up of new land; and repair and maintenance of public buildings, machinery, and equipment.

The search for improved living standards must be accompanied by an attempt to increase exports so as to afford vital imports, without reliance on external finance, which will probably be unavailable and may be undesirable.

Such activities adapt very favourably, and at low cost, to the large-scale use and organization of labour, and it is this quality which recommends their adoption in the present circumstances. At the same time, such activities imply a break with the dominant style of development, as they seek to restore the importance of a labour process aimed at satisfying essential needs and fully using the labour force and other under-utilized potential, while making less use of scarce factors, such as capital and foreign inputs. Moreover, these activities give rise to a different style of development and a more vigorous and open local cultural identity. As a result of the multiple links which connect them with specific geographical contexts, with daily experience, and with local knowledge and culture, as well as with the relationships which make up the natural ecosystems, these opportunities tend to be adopted more within an emergency framework. It is consequently vital to take advantage of the period of crisis which began in 1982 to identify and quickly to stimulate activities such as those mentioned above.

In most cases, these activities involve collective consumption or the utilization and expansion of productive infrastructure, not always of interest to private enterprise. This is either because the investments required will only be profitable in the long term, because they are for the benefit of low-income sectors whose effective demand is very modest, or because the purpose is to create external economies, or to avoid external diseconomies whose benefits the private investor is not able to reap. In other words, these are activities and undertakings which normally fall within the sphere of responsibility of the public sector.

Another of the principal features of these activities and projects is their localized geographical specificity. The problem of unemployment and that of the utilization, conservation, protection, and improvement of the natural and built environment are not abstract concepts, but take on their true meaning in relation to concrete places and localities, especially in countries which have extremely heterogeneous and varied environments. In consequence, this is a field of public interest which is particularly suitable for decentralization and community participation, both of which are points of special interest and priority in the search for democratic planning and decision-making systems. While the circumstances surrounding the crisis may act as a detonator to set off this type of movement, the fact that it concerns essential and widespread needs which have been systematically ignored suggests the opportunity to set up such programmes as permanent features of development, with adequate institutional and financial backing, and with a medium- and long-term outlook.

In this respect, a priority area for readjustment of development patterns, as pointed out earlier, must be that relating to the patterns of consumption and investment, as well as the options chosen in the fields of technology and resource management. It will be essential to impose severe and selective restrictions, save in the most exceptional circumstances, on all types of superfluous demand which directly or indirectly involve a high imported element, and on all technology or designs which have the same implications, while promoting efforts to replace them by goods and services, technologies, and designs which rely on the use of national and local human and material resources, essentially aimed at satisfying basic needs.

All of the lines of action suggested above involve greater pressure upon the environment. The expansion, preservation, maintenance, and protection of the environmental heritage consequently represents a fundamental contribution to standards of living and productivity. This necessarily implies greater awareness of its potential, of the ecosystemic conditioning factors which determine its exploitation, and of the most efficient ways of managing it, with the aim of making maximum use of the opportunities it offers, but avoiding exhausting and damaging it, so as to ensure its long-term maintenance. All this implies the need to give priority in any future development plans to the theme of natural resources and science and technology, adopting an ecological and long-term view. In short, it is a question of becoming fully aware of the theme of the material sustainability of development.

Stressing the exploitation of indigenous resources means making a greater distinction than in the past between and within countries. It requires that in development strategies we should come down from an exaggerated level of abstraction to a concrete examination of the available natural resources and technology, the size and position of the country, the relationship between the population and resources, the position as far as energy is concerned, and the degree and features of urbanization. This means that the new development strategies will necessarily have to be different for countries which show marked differences in these features. It also implies that such strategies will have to pay special attention to regional and spatial aspects (including the urban–rural theme), since we have to deal with resources of varying capacity and use, that consequently involve diverse technologies, with different levels of knowledge and methods of application—all of which is in sharp contrast with the homogenizing tendencies which have been imposed upon a whole variety of features: crops, technologies, architectural design, administrative norms and standards, and consumption patterns.

The planning methodology which has been followed in the past, and in particular the secondary role allowed to the state in recent years, under neoliberal influence, has paid little attention to these considerations, largely because—just like the development strategies themselves—this methodology was considerably influenced by an approach fundamentally based on the imitation of the patterns of consumption and development of the industrialized countries, and relying to an extreme degree upon the national and international market.

One of the difficulties affecting coordination between short- and longer-term development policies lies in the fact that short-term economic policy falls within the sphere of influence of the economists and managers of the ministries of finance and the central banks, while development planning, programmes, and projects are the responsibility of planning agencies, quasi-autonomous state enterprises responsible for energy and natural resources, and the ministries responsible for public works, regional and urban development, education, science and technology, and the productive and social sectors of the economy. An institutional solution must be provided which will improve coordination between short-term management and long-term development planning.

A final remark concerns the distinction between short- and long-term policies, which is of great importance in attempting to face both the recession and the structural crisis. At first sight, long-term policies—such as those which affect preservation of the environment and natural resources, population, education, science and technology, international relations, and modes of social organization —would appear to bear little relation to short-term problems. But, as we have attempted to make clear, such policies are rich in opportunities for helping to solve some of these short-term problems, for example, not only in job creation, satisfying basic needs, but also in developing new exports and replacing imports. On the other hand, conjunctural policies, designed to react in the face of recession, may be designed to preserve and improve social and productive structures and facilities in the long term, instead of accentuating their waste and deterioration. Consequently, close collaboration between those who are concerned with short-term disequilibria and those whose task it is to consider medium- and long-term development may be worthwhile and fruitful in so far as both bear in mind the need to achieve *sustainable development*.

Past experience, both recent and more remote, has provided examples of development strategies and policies which, with hindsight, have proved to be unsustainable, and which have led to deep crises. Our economic and social history is marked by cycles of boom and slump based upon the exploitation of particularly favourable natural resources.

The most recent cycle in the Southern Cone has been both the most remarkable and the most regrettable: it has been remarkable in so far as it was based upon the export of a myth—confidence in the miraculous capacities of the free market economy (domestic and external) to exploit our resources; it has been regrettable, in so far as it has led to the heavy over-exploitation of certain resources and to areas of acute environmental damage, to severe social and economic backwardness, and moreover to external (and domestic) indebtedness of outstandingly serious proportions. These features weigh heavily upon the possibilities of future growth and development.

During the next decades, Latin America will be obliged to generate such enormous trade surpluses that its potential for economic growth will be for the most part transferred beyond its frontiers, leaving little hope of recovering and even less of improving the standard of living and level of employment which existed a decade and a half ago, or even of reducing the burden of the external debt. If international conditions were to improve, Latin American countries would be able to face a more promising and comforting future. However, it is unlikely that the international economy will provide us with such a favourable set of conditions in the next decade. In these circumstances, it would seem advisable to examine the debt problem in a radically different way, as we suggested in the previous chapter; but such a reexamination would imply different domestic and international political conditions from those which exist at present and, above all, more joint action on the part of the debtor countries.

Even in the best possible circumstances, it will not be possible for future development to rely, as in the past, on the massive contribution of external resources. On the contrary, it is highly likely that additional net external financing will be in extremely short supply in future years. In simple terms, dollars will be hard to come by and it will be increasingly necessary to ration their use, be it by new successive devaluations and/or by exchange and import control, or, most probably, by both. In addition, the time will come when it will be impossible to continue importing luxury cars, electrical and electronic appliances, liquor, and other luxury goods when there is a shortage of food and other essential goods or raw materials.

Economic policy will increasingly stress the development of exports and import substitution, as well as especially stimulating production of the most essential goods and services. Future development cannot be on an 'easy terms' basis. These countries will have to become genuinely self-sufficient to a substantial degree; they will have to grow basically with their own means, their own natural resources, their own environmental conditions, and their own capacity for work, inventiveness, technology, and organization, including the development of a capability of penetrating the world markets selectively. Whatever external contribution proves necessary will be complementary and selective, and no longer predominant and directive. They must adjust themselves to this new reality, or irreversibly tear themselves apart. Either their own limited resources will be divided up among the entire population, after having ensured a high level of savings and accumulation, or else an increasingly isolated minority will manage for some time to maintain a standard of living similar to that of the industrialized countries, surrounded by the immense and ever-growing majority of an unemployed, marginal, and poor population, who will not allow them to enjoy this privilege for long.

There is an enormous task implied in the renewed challenge of sustainable development. Sustainable development requires an adequate level of accumulation, efficiency, and creativity; in the social sphere, a reasonable margin of equity and opportunities for work and a decent standard of living; in the international sphere, acceptance as respectable members of the community of nations, and the capacity to maintain satisfactory international relationships; in the sphere of human rights, respect for the basic rights of the individual, the family, and the basic social organizations; in the cultural sphere, the achievement, on the one hand, of a certain level of identity with an adherence to the best values and traditions which make up and distinguish our nations and, on the other, the necessary creativity and selectivity to overcome our problems and to attain our sociocultural aims; in the political sphere, the attainment and maintenance of an acceptable degree of legitimacy, renewal, and representativity of the authorities, and participation by the people in the institutions which govern them; in the environmental sphere, the certainty that the environmental and natural resources inherited from the past will be handed down to future generations under the best possible conditions of awareness, use, and conservation or replacement, so as to ensure that they provide an improved material basis for the survival and well-being of those generations.

Notes

1. The link between the transfer problem and the internal adjustment is seen in the macroeconomic identity which links domestic adjustment to external adjustment:

   $$M - X + R = I - SN$$

   where

   $M - X$ = trade balance
   R = net factor payments (made up mainly of interest payments)
   I = total investment
   SN = national savings

For a useful discussion of this relationship and its evolution during recent years for the major Latin American economies, see Inter-American Development Bank, *Economic and Social Progress in Latin America*, 1985 Report, Washington, DC.

2. Quoted in *El Mercurio*, Santiago, 30 October 1984.

Index